Quarto
Knows

Inspiring | Educating | Creating | Entertaining

Brimming with creative inspiration, how-to projects, and useful information to enrich your everyday life, Quarto Knows is a favorite destination for those pursuing their interests and passions. Visit our site and dig deeper with our books into your area of interest: Quarto Creates, Quarto Cooks, Quarto Homes, Quarto Lives, Quarto Drives, Quarto Explores, Quarto Gifts, or Quarto Kids.

10 9 8 7 6 5 4 3 2 1

ISBN: 978-1-63106-736-5

Library of Congress Cataloging-in-Publication Data

Names: Kuchta, Alyssa, author.
Title: Follow your bliss : wisdom from inspiring women to help you find purpose and joy / Alyssa Kuchta.
Description: New York, NY : Rock Point, an imprint of The Quarto Group, 2021. | Summary: "Follow your Bliss is a gorgeous book filled with powerful advice from aspirational women for go-getters from all stages of life"-- Provided by publisher.
Identifiers: LCCN 2021005053 (print) | LCCN 2021005054 (ebook) | ISBN 9781631067365 (hardcover) | ISBN 9780760369593 (ebook)
Subjects: LCSH: Businesswomen--Quotations.
Classification: LCC HD6054.3 .K83 2021 (print) | LCC HD6054.3 (ebook) | DDC 650.092/52--dc23
LC record available at https://lccn.loc.gov/2021005053
LC ebook record available at https://lccn.loc.gov/2021005054

Publisher: Rage Kindelsperger
Creative Director: Laura Drew
Managing Editor: Cara Donaldson
Editor: Keyla Pizarro-Hernández
Cover and Interior Design: Evelin Kasikov

Printed in China

This book provides general information on various widely known and widely accepted images that tend to evoke feelings of strength and confidence. However, it should not be relied upon as recommending or promoting any specific diagnosis or method of treatment for a particular condition, and it is not intended as a substitute for medical advice or for direct diagnosis and treatment of a medical condition by a qualified physician. Readers who have questions about a particular condition, possible treatments for that condition, or possible reactions from the condition or its treatment should consult a physician or other qualified healthcare professional.

FOLLOW YOUR BLISS

Wisdom from Inspiring Women to Help You Find Purpose and Joy

ALYSSA KUCHTA

ROCK POINT

Acknowledgments

I want to thank Rage Kindelsperger for believing in me and offering the opportunity to bring this book into the world. This has been an experience of a lifetime!

To the women I had the honor of interviewing for this book, thank you from the bottom of my heart for courageously sharing your stories and being shining examples to others of what it means to *follow your bliss.*

To my editor, Keyla Pizzaro-Hernández, for her incredible writing guidance through this process and bringing this book to life.

To my mom, who has always been a shining example of what it means to be a fierce, independent, strong woman. Everything I am, I owe to you.

To my husband, Sam, my soul mate, biggest cheerleader, and support system. I couldn't imagine my life without you.

To my gang of ladies—Natasha, Maxine, Olivia, Jordan, Megan, Raisa, and Catherine—who helped me power through creating this book. Your friendships mean the world to me.

To my f.y.b team and customers, who inspire me and keep me going every day. Words could never express my gratitude for you.

To my readers, thank you for choosing this book to help guide you on your journey. My greatest wish is that this book helps you feel inspired and empowered to follow your own bliss in life, and know through these stories that your dreams *are* possible and success can mean so many different things. Your journey is up to you.

TABLE OF CONTENTS

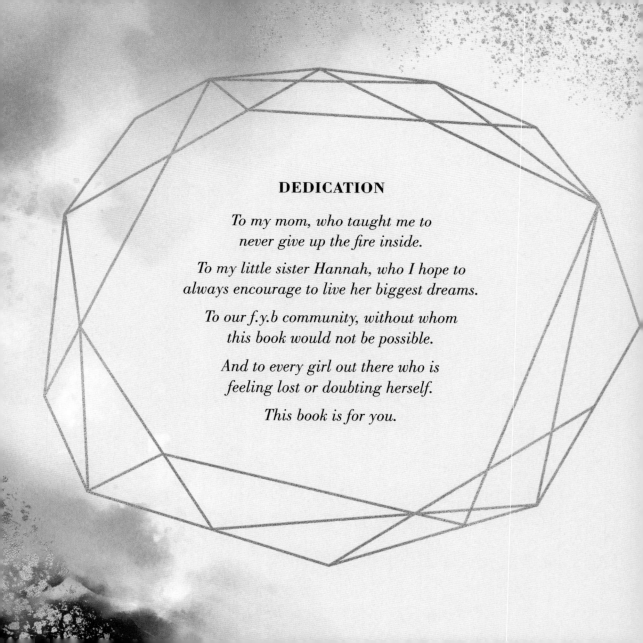

DEDICATION

*To my mom, who taught me to
never give up the fire inside.*

*To my little sister Hannah, who I hope to
always encourage to live her biggest dreams.*

*To our f.y.b community, without whom
this book would not be possible.*

*And to every girl out there who is
feeling lost or doubting herself.*

This book is for you.

INTRODUCTION

I started f.y.b jewelry in 2011 with less than $100 in my bank account, a big dream, and a little moxie on my side. It was a leap of faith into a future that I hadn't planned for. I was a rising senior in college and experienced what I refer to as a "mid-college" crisis. I was graduating in a year and realized I had spent most of my college years on autopilot, pursuing a major and a life path I didn't actually want.

———— • ————

I found myself daydreaming off in my classes, feeling intimidated by my friends who had their careers figured out and jobs lined up, and experiencing overwhelming anxiety about my future. I wasn't focusing on the things that made me feel alive. I wasn't following my bliss. This feeling of utter confusion led to my biggest breakthrough. It pushed me to search within myself, to take a breath and a step back and ask, "What do I *really* want?" and "What am I *truly* passionate about?"

Launching my business was the moment in my life when I gave in to the flow of my own happiness. It ignited my entrepreneurial spirit, pushed me far beyond my comfort zone, taught me to be resourceful and resilient, and gave me hope that I could build a life and path of my choosing. I've worked hard ever since to build the company into not just a jewelry brand, but also a space for women to gather and feel supported. From our brand ambassador program, where I've been able to mentor and create a powerful network of hundreds of young women over the years, to selling our collections with nationwide retail partners, my own journey has been proof that you can change your course, make an impact, and bring your vision to life no matter what obstacles stand in your way.

Following your bliss is so much more than just doing what makes you happy. It's about trusting your intuition, living a life with passion and purpose, and not allowing yourself to settle for less. It's self-love and acceptance, challenging yourself and pushing beyond your comfort zones, making yourself proud, and discovering *who you are*.

Growing up the daughter of a Chinese immigrant mother and a father with an undiagnosed mental illness, I had a childhood filled with financial hardships, volatility, and change. I dealt with a lot of shame around my identity and home life. During these times, my mother was always the shining example of what it means to be fierce and independent. Her perseverance through endless adversity has always been living proof to me of what a woman can accomplish if she has enough grit, purpose, and determination to pull her through.

She built a rich and fulfilling life for herself and her children. She showed me that the things that I was ashamed of were all part of my story, and they've led me to be the woman I am today: a proud biracial entrepreneur and business owner, with a mission to spread joy and make the world a little bit brighter. I want f.y.b jewelry to be the beacon of light my mother was to me. I want it to encourage women to embrace who they are, where they come from, and whatever dreams they long to chase.

I believe the most powerful way to inspire others is to *show* them what's possible. This book is a compilation of stories and advice from sixty inspiring, trailblazing women from all different life stages, backgrounds, and fields. I spent a year conducting interviews and connecting with women ranging from up-and-coming entrepreneurs to groundbreaking activists, Grammy award-winning musicians, and U.S. Olympians; these revolutionary women have come together to offer their wisdom and guidance. While they all have a different story to tell, the one thing that they have in common is that they have all chosen to *follow their bliss*. They have all had the courage to take the road less traveled, to own who they are, and to get back up no matter how many times they are knocked down.

My hope is that you, the reader, will find inspiration in hearing these tales of triumph born from adversity, like an arrow being pulled back before release, and find the confidence to fly through the air toward your target; to follow your bliss with the power of sisterhood behind you. Even the most successful women have gone through setbacks and moments of self-doubt.

This book is proof that there is no one-size-fits-all decision when it comes to our chosen paths. Our bliss, our purpose, and our happiness are what we make them. There is beauty in the struggle. We often find ourselves in the moments when we are pushed to persevere, to ride the wave, to think positive, to be a wing woman. These are the meanings behind the charms in the f.y.b collection. They are the little messages we all need to hear sometimes to summon the spirit and bravery to keep going.

Let this book be your guide. In moments of self-doubt, anxiety, or fear, pick it up and read a chapter or two. Let the stories of these women help you feel less alone. Let the lives they've lived inspire you to take a deeper look inside yourself and reassess what is truly important. Our stories, hardships, and experiences are what make us interesting and uniquely us. When you're feeling out of balance: inhale confidence, love, and support, and exhale fear and any feelings that are not serving you.

Life is full of peaks and valleys and wherever you are on your journey is exactly where you need to be. Take in the intrinsic magic around you and trust that you have the power to create something truly special. We all have a story to tell: make yours one for the books. Follow your bliss and trust that the journey will be wildly, joyously, *imperfectly* perfect.

LIVE INSPIRED

Everything begins from a moment of inspiration.

Everything that is and will ever be begins from a moment of inspiration. We are constantly surrounded by endless sources of inspiration, we just have to choose to notice them. Perhaps it's a page in a magazine that inspires the color palette of your next collection, a heartbreak that inspires the love story in your first screenplay, or a volunteer experience that inspires you to join or launch a nonprofit organization—inspiration can be drawn from the smallest of moments to the most profound experiences, and it's up to us to let these sparkling strobes of brilliance in.

———— • ————

Sometimes feeling lost, lacking inspiration, and not knowing where to begin can be the biggest blessing in disguise. It forces you to shake things up, to think deeply about who you are and what you actually want, to do things differently than you've done before, to explore. Not knowing where to begin is actually the *best place* to begin; you can start with a clean slate. When things are unknown, anything is possible.

This was exactly the case for me. I had no idea what I wanted to do after graduating college. I thought I would follow the path my mom hoped for me and become a psychologist, but I felt in my gut that I was meant for something else. I went through a period of major soul searching, getting involved in as many things as I could. I also spent hours sitting on my bed with a notebook listing out activities I enjoyed, people I admired, hopes I had for myself, and tried to make sense of it all.

As I spent time drawing inspiration from the things around me and the things inside of me, the light bulb for launching my own brand began to illuminate and my passions became clearer. The dots begin to connect when you reflect, and you realize the signs guiding you to your purpose were there all along.

Living inspired means paying attention to the things that excite you, the things that give you butterflies, the things that make you a little more curious about the world. Start with a pen and a notebook and write down your ideas, moments of creative inspiration, thoughts, and interests. The more you write things out, the easier it is for these things to start connecting.

When you're feeling uninspired, get out in nature, stroll through your favorite shops and bookstores, listen to music, browse through magazines, brainstorm with friends, and reflect on the experiences in your own life from which you can pull inspiration.

Inspiration is everywhere and anywhere we choose to seek it, and it often happens in the moments we are still and present.

"Life is about taking risks.
If you play your life safe and you don't take risks, you're going to live your life at a low hum. That might be fine for certain people, but I don't want to live my life at a low hum. I want to live my life proud and loud and to the fullest expression that I possibly can."

ROBBIE BRENNER

Oscar®-nominated Producer,
Executive VP and Producer, Mattel Films

AS A YOUNG GIRL growing up in Manhattan, Robbie had a love for movies and storytelling. After graduating from NYU Tisch School of the Arts, Robbie moved to Los Angeles on a whim on New Year's Eve with just a bag of clothes in her possession and no plan. She knew she had to take the leap and make her dreams come true. She ended up working as a personal assistant to Mickey Rourke and eventually landed a job at Miramax, where she hustled working and reading scripts. Robbie read and pushed a script called *Boondock Saints* that went on to be a successful film, and Miramax promoted her for her eye and work ethic.

Robbie has gone on to produce and work on some of the most successful films in Hollywood, such as *Serendipity*, *Haven*, and *Alien vs. Predator*. One of her most notable films is the Academy Award–winning *Dallas Buyers Club*. Believing in stories that weren't immediately accepted are risks that have led to some of her greatest accolades.

For Robbie, the most inspiring people are the ones who take risks. When you're teetering on the edge of success and failure, amazing things can happen. Find things that excite you and go for them. Follow your instincts. Who knows? Maybe that move across the country, that spark from your childhood, or the friends you make along the way will change your life forever.

"You need to listen to your gut and go at your own pace. There's a ton of wisdom in previous ways of doing things, but it's also always changing and evolving. How you approach things needs to be entirely your own."

DIANNA COHEN

Founder and CEO of Crown Affair

AFTER HIGH SCHOOL, Dianna moved to Manhattan to study art history and marketing at NYU, then worked at Into the Gloss and Away, Spring, and Tamara Mellon. Dianna's work kept her traveling, and she was constantly disappointed in the hotel hair products, which led her to realize the gap in the market for quality hair products focused on ritual.

She began sharing her advice and product reviews on a Google Doc with friends, and that spread like wildfire. She realized that many women were disconnected from this part of their beauty routine. She had inadvertently created a community and by looking at hair care through a branding lens, she realized a business concept she was eager to launch.

Taking inspiration from Japanese art and minimalism, her favorite films, and color palettes from book covers and paintings, the aesthetic for her company, Crown Affair, began to emerge. Launched in January 2020, Crown Affair has become a successful company blazing a new trail for the hair product industry.

Every step of Dianna's journey inspired and prepared her for the entrepreneurial path she has today. You never know how that internship, job, mentor, or moment of inspiration will impact you down the road. When you're feeling stuck, find something you can do that connects you back to the self. For Dianna, that means stretching, writing in her journal, or going to a museum. Honor your body and mind and inspiration will follow.

"To me, living inspired is being open to the idea that all opportunities and stories can leave an impact on you, and that all the stories you share can equally leave a lasting impact on others."

AMBER VITTORIA

Inspiring Artist and Illustrator

EVERY LITTLE STORY in your life can have a lasting impact on how you move forward, whether it's a struggle or an opportunity—everything is a lesson for you to carry with you for next time. Amber's inspiration came from using her experiences as valuable tools for living a life full of purpose. For Amber, it was her struggles—such as her complications with reproductive health, being objectified on the street, and being paid less at work than she deserved—that led her to create authentic artwork about womanhood. Her multifaceted art pieces aim to paint the stories of womanhood as the complex, relatable, and honest stories that they are, while dismantling limiting societal tropes. She has collaborated with the likes of the *New York Times*, Warby Parker, and Gucci.

It's hard to work in an industry that favors men, but Amber finds joy and encouragement in the fact that many people connect to her art on a personal level. Even when the industry makes it harder for her, she continues to find ways to inspire others.

Beyond artwork, living a life that you want has everything to do with how you use inspiration to move through decisions and propel yourself forward. Amber used her struggles as inspiration to build her incredible career. Don't let your struggles or challenges stop you from living the life you envision. Every moment is a beautiful story that you can use to keep going and encourage others to do so as well.

BE
BOLD

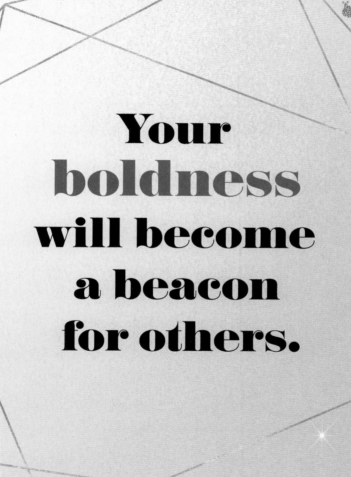

Your boldness will become a beacon for others.

It's easy to get caught up in the little worries of day-to-day life. We worry about the judgment of others. We worry we're not good enough. We worry we won't be able to pull off that red lipstick. Being bold means letting go of the things that don't serve us. It means stepping out of the status quo with vision and purpose. Boldness isn't a given: it's a choice. We can choose to stay small and comfortable or we can step out of our comfort zone and experience everything the world has to offer.

———— • ————

I've been lucky to have strong female role models in my life, from my mother, who made the bold decision of being the first in her family to emigrate to the United States from China, to the incredible network of women I've surrounded myself with throughout my career and aspire to emulate—activists, leaders, entrepreneurs—to the women featured right here in this book. Boldness is in their blood. They've galvanized me to choose the life I want to lead, rather than go along with what is expected.

Being bold for me meant stepping out on my own and choosing to start a jewelry brand, regardless of the difficulties or competitiveness of the market. This bold decision was about not listening to the doubts of others, and trusting my inner voice that I was capable of success. Being bold means being imaginative and seeing what others cannot yet see. It's about defining who you are underneath the layers and societal norms that have been placed on you.

What's something that scares you? Perhaps it's starting that business you've always dreamed of, speaking out about something you believe in, or wearing that one dress in your closet that you stare at longingly every morning. Don't let fear hold you back. Live in your truth, and have the confidence and courage to take a stand for something you believe in. Be a voice for others. Stand up to injustice. Know your worth, what you're capable of, and don't let self-doubt creep in.

Find one thing that matters to you in this life, find one thing that you wish you could change, and take the first step towards it. We all have the power to make a difference in this world, no matter how big or how small our efforts.

Go after your dreams. Be bold knowing that there is a sisterhood of freethinking, strong women right beside you. Put on the dress. Make the time you have on this planet the most paradigm-shattering, unforgettable years you possibly can, because a bold woman doesn't leave a legacy by being like everyone else.

"**Being bold is to say the things I know are true but am terrified to say. Truthfulness is bold.**"

CONNIE LIM, A.K.A. MILCK

Empowering Singer-Songwriter

CONNIE'S PARENTS MOVED to the United States from China to offer Connie and her sister a better life, and Connie felt a heavy weight to be successful in order to justify their sacrifice. She worked extremely hard in school to succeed in fields that didn't fit her creative personality. She only felt free and calm when she was creating music. It was through her music that she was able to live in her truth.

In letting out her struggles and unique experiences through her songs, she's found a deeper connection with her listeners. This sentiment was even more apparent when her song "Quiet" became the anthem of the 2017 Women's March. Her performance at the march received over eight million views in just two days, catapulting Connie, known in music as MILCK, to stardom and a deal with Atlantic Records.

Being bold for Connie has meant unshackling herself from the weight of expectation and creating music with clarity. The honesty of Connie's story drew others in and created a space for women to speak about issues that may have gone unspoken. Sharing and connecting with others has tremendous power; it emboldens us to be free, to express ourselves in the purest form. Speak out and let your voice be heard. You never know who might be listening.

"Women that I admire have untethered from cultural norms, they've untethered from societal expectations, they've untethered sometimes from people. And that radical idea of women being able to walk away and experience freedom, complete freedom, is, to me, the essence of being bold."

JODIE PATTERSON

Board Director of the Human Rights Campaign,
LGBTQAI Advocate, Author, and Entrepreneur

ACTIVISM, IN ITS purest sense, is in Jodie's blood. Her uncle, Gil Scott-Heron, famously wrote the poem and song "The Revolution Will Not Be Televised," and her mother started the Patterson School, a nonprofit, multicultural, and nondenominational private school in Harlem.

The power of her family's motivation to take courageous action peaked some years into Jodie's time as a mother. Everything changed for Jodie when one of her children came out as transgender. She took time to listen and understand her son in order to better provide a happy life for him. In doing so, she expanded the reach of her compassion, adaptability, and knowledge. This expansion has served Jodie in her own journey to finding her truest self.

She has also found that the change brought on by her divorce has challenged her to find a deeper expression of self, beyond just mother and wife. Stepping out of our obligations allows us to see more clearly who we are outside of the expectation of others.

Think about the things and people that are important to you and how you measure your worth. What do you use to define yourself? Once you recognize these defining areas of your life, you have to untether yourself from them in order to find who you truly are. Let go of expectations and find the truest expression of *you*. There is nothing bolder than a woman fearlessly living in her independence.

"**Abandon all the expectations everyone has of you and any ambition of being perfect.** Use your incredibly powerful voice. Even if it makes others uncomfortable. *Especially* if it makes others uncomfortable."

MANDANA DAYANI

*Creator and Cofounder of I Am a Voter,
Cohost of The Dissenters Podcast,
Attorney, and Angel Investor*

AS AN IMMIGRANT and a religious refugee, Mandana has always had a deep understanding and respect for the privilege it is to be an American. In the wake of the 2016 election, she was heartbroken to see the growing division in our country. She had just given birth to her daughter, Miller, and was seeing young children being taken from their parents at the border. She wanted to ease the tension in the discourse and find solutions.

After some research, where she discovered that one hundred million registered voters didn't vote in 2016, Mandana decided to direct her focus to voter turnout. Mandana cofounded I Am a Voter with the bold idea of rebranding voter participation in America. Her nonpartisan organization works to energize citizens to engage in our democracy in a new and inviting way. Mandana's podcast, *The Dissenters*, which she cohosts with her best friend, actor and philanthropist Debra Messing, is an extension of her work as an activist. Together, they interview twenty of their heroes who challenged the status quo to build a better way, in an effort to prove that everyone can find their purpose and create meaningful change.

Taking bold action when you feel something isn't right is an important part of what it means to be an activist. To Mandana, it takes honesty, courage, hope, and commitment to your community. Don't ask for permission to be yourself. Don't worry about disappointing others. You choose the legacy you leave behind, so be bold to protect and honor it.

SELF
LOVE

The love we have for ourselves sets the bar for all the other love we experience. It starts with us.

Love begins with us. We can get so caught up in seeking validation from others that we forget the most important love is the love we have for ourselves. Knowing our worth and valuing who we are and how we treat ourselves sets the bar for how others will treat us. To love ourselves is to not settle for less than we deserve; it's prioritizing healthy habits and self-care, striving to show up as the best possible version of ourselves, and knowing we must fill our own cup before we can fill others'.

Do things that expand your mind, body, and soul. Set aside nonnegotiable "me" time each week to reset yourself, whether it's a weekly bubble bath with a glass of wine, journaling, trying a new recipe, or getting out in nature. When you're feeling off, shake things up. Identify and change your unhealthy patterns. Listen to your body and take it as a sign you need to rest and reset.

When you're in an insecure and negative space, you won't attract anything good into your life. Self-love is learning to only compare yourself with who you were yesterday. It's saying "no" and having boundaries, not spreading yourself thin. Take note of how you're spending your time and whether you're doing things that help or hurt your mental state.

Growing up as a biracial girl in a school that lacked diversity greatly shaped my formative years. The lack of representation of Asian women in both film and media, and limited societal standards of beauty, impacted my self-esteem and the way I saw myself. I never felt that I fit in and I rarely felt beautiful through much of my adolescent years. I became so fixated on trying to fit in and look like everyone else that I failed to see myself for who I really was.

It wasn't until I went to college that I felt confident in myself. It was being outside of my comfort bubble and being immersed in diversity, surrounding myself with loving and supportive friends, and discovering my passions and who I was, that led me to my own path of self-love and acceptance.

Beauty is more than skin deep—beauty is in the way you treat people, the care you give others, and the work you put out into the world. Beauty comes in all shapes and sizes. Remember, you tell the world who *you* are, not the other way around.

You are worthy of your own love. Love yourself even on your worst days because you—yes, *you*—are enough no matter what. When you own who you are, that's when the magic happens.

"I can't control my body, but I absolutely have the power to control my thoughts. Life doesn't always give you what you want. But it gives you what you need, to mold you, to hurt you, and to gradually strengthen you into the person you were meant to become."

GAYLYN HENDERSON

Founder of Gutless and Glamorous

AFTER BEING DIAGNOSED with Crohn's disease at the age of fourteen, Gaylyn struggled for many years with the discomfort, and at times debilitating pain, of a chronic illness. When your body is keeping you from living, and enjoying, in the most basic sense, it's easy to lose hope. Gaylyn found herself fearful of moving forward with ostomy surgery, despite the possibility of positive and life-changing benefits.

Ultimately, she found strength and love within, and powered through the surgery with optimism on her side. Her only regret? Not doing it sooner. This is why Gaylyn founded Gutless and Glamorous, a nonprofit organization dedicated to removing the stigma around ostomy for those living with or considering the surgery. She didn't want anyone to shy away from treatment because of their own self-judgment or preconceived notions. Gaylyn has learned to remain constant in not letting the beliefs of others control how she views herself, and that true beauty can only come from within. What she has been through has only made her stronger.

It is easy to look at our challenges or what we view as our faults and feel unworthy. But loving yourself isn't about achieving perfection. If you learn to find love for your greatest gifts as well as your deepest insecurities, you'll awaken your full confidence; by doing so, you'll lift up the people around you to do the same.

"I didn't see myself represented in the media as a little girl. Having the opportunity to be the representation I needed as a child means the world to me. Knowing that **I can potentially make a difference and inspire other girls who felt like they didn't fit in is what keeps me going.**"

DANI CANDRAY

Model, Alopecian Advocate and Mentor

DANI WAS DIAGNOSED with alopecia at just two and a half years old. As a child, Dani hadn't fully grasped the effect alopecia would have on her life. After being bullied in school and not seeing women who looked like her represented in the media, she struggled with the desire to feel normal. The idea of going without her wig seemed insurmountable. She recalls feeling worthless without her hair, and despite having the support of her loved ones, she felt alone. With the encouragement of her mother, Dani attended a conference for the National Alopecia Areata Foundation (NAAF) and began connecting with the alopecia community.

Upon meeting other people like her, Dani embarked on a journey to deeper self-love, confidence, and appreciation. The NAAF conference inspired her to stop hiding who she was. She decided to take her sophomore yearbook photo without her wig on and embrace her natural beauty. She has since gone on to model for companies like Aerie and continues her advocacy and mentorship for those struggling with alopecia. Dani is fueled by knowing she can potentially make a difference and inspire other women to discover their own self-worth.

Self-love is a journey. It's okay to feel insecure sometimes, but don't let those insecurities define your experiences. You are unique. Find your tribe and surround yourself with others who see the beauty in you. With time and intention, you can accomplish things that may have previously felt impossible.

"Being beautiful
can mean so many things,
and I think that's something
young girls need to know. You
need to love yourself on every level.
When you find confidence in
your insecurities, you start
to love all of yourself."

JESSICA IACULLO

Founder of Hungry Jess Big City

FOR JESSICA, BEING a teenager was not easy. She felt insecure in her curvy body. It wasn't until college, and discovering a passion for self-expression through writing, that Jessica began to embrace the parts of her that made her different. The first personal article she wrote was about wanting a breast reduction but deciding not to get one. This article went viral and resonated with a lot of women. The feeling of connection and community she received through being open, honest, and vulnerable is what propelled her forward with her writing.

She began to value herself beyond just her physical body. In forming a new relationship with her own opinions, ways of thinking, and connections with people, she expanded her definition of self-worth. She realized that love extends beyond the romantic form. You can be loved for, and have love for, your creativity, your talents, your contributions, and your passions. Out of Jessica's expansion of self-love and discovery, her digital platform, Hungry Jess Big City, was born. Think sassy snark combined with foodie heart, Hungry Jess Big City is all about inspiring your next meal, adventure, or major life change. Jessica has since landed collaborations with the likes of *Cosmopolitan*, Food Network chefs, and *Forbes*, to name a few.

Self-awareness is where our path to self-love and confidence begins. It becomes a journey of not letting others' judgments define you, learning to love who you are, and opening yourself to passions and interests that help you expand into the best possible version of yourself.

Saying yes
opens your heart,
mind, and spirit to
a world of possibilities
beyond what you
imagined.

I moved to New York City in 2014. I was twenty-three years old, and in the infant stages of growing my business. I had been living at home with my parents after college, keeping expenses lean and saving money. I didn't have a stable income yet, but I knew that I needed to make a big change if I wanted momentous growth, personally and professionally. So I pushed myself to take a leap and move out of state. I felt that this move would force me to figure things out. I said "yes" before I felt ready, and said "yes" to shaking things up even though I was scared.

Sometimes you have to jump in, say "yes," and figure things out afterward. Pushing yourself to these "sink or swim" moments is sometimes the necessary fire you need to kick things into high gear. In my first few years living in NYC, there was *nothing* I'd say "no" to. Whether it was a networking event, a pop-up opportunity, a date, or a spontaneous dinner with new people, I pushed myself out of every comfort zone with a hunger to experience and connect with others. My early twenties were an adventure of meeting incredible people who opened my mind and heart in so many ways.

When you live your life with a "yes" mentality, you open your mind, heart, and spirit to a world of possibilities beyond what you imagined. Every person is a door to a new world, and every person you'll ever meet knows something that you don't. Say "yes" to that blind date, that chance to study abroad, that event you're nervous to attend alone, that internship or job opportunity in a new city. One day you'll look back and connect the dots and see how every experience led to another that got you to where you are today.

Say "no" to people who don't recognize your worth, to things that don't excite you, to limiting yourself, to not feeling worthy. Establish your own set of nonnegotiables for the life you want to live, and set out with a "yes" mentality to allow better things to follow suit.

The most interesting people have gotten where they are because they said "yes" at some point in time to something out of their comfort zone. What can you say "yes" to that you've been avoiding or not feeling ready for?

In saying "yes" to new experiences, you'll discover new passions, explore the things that interest you, and allow yourself to live a life filled with love and adventure.

"You can't make a wrong choice, everything will inform. There are no wrongs. On the other side of fear is oftentimes connection and self-esteem. You're worth it. We're capable of doing things that are really uncomfortable."

TAYLOR SCHILLING

Award-winning Actor, Golden Globe Nominee

TAYLOR GREW UP in Boston, Massachusetts, in a tumultuous home environment. When Taylor was fourteen, her parents formally separated, and she went to live with a family friend. During that time, Taylor started to meet people whom she regards as "little angels guiding her on her path." Her high school drama teachers encouraged her to audition for college drama programs.

Taylor has gone on to star as the leading role in the hit Netflix series *Orange Is the New Black*, for which she received a Primetime Emmy nomination and two Golden Globe nominations. She has had a highly successful career starring in television and film projects, such as *Argo*, *The Overnight*, and *The Prodigy*.

A big part of Taylor's success has been saying yes to the things that make her uncomfortable. She's found that often the most challenging opportunities end up being the most gratifying. For her, the scary unknowns are her north star. Taylor has learned that even though the audition process is difficult, she really does enjoy the ride. Her creative life is the result of saying yes to big, risky things and working hard to make them prosper.

She encourages everyone to see what they can do for others. We are all living in the imperfect human experience, so say yes to being vulnerable with the people in your life and harness the love born out of connection. Love will always make you stronger.

"What began as a
'what am I doing and why
am I here?' moment transformed
into resiliency and knowing that I
could take care of myself. I think young
people should do the Peace Corps or other
service or experience to get out of their
comfort zone. Throughout the process,
**you grow in ways you would
never expect to.**"

SUSAN ROCKEFELLER

Entrepreneur, Conservationist, and Filmmaker

AFTER COLLEGE, SUSAN made the unconventional decision to travel and live with the Inuit in the Arctic, learning firsthand how to live off the land and be in harmony with nature. She struggled with the difficult task of working in agriculture in a climate where the growing season is a mere three months, but she integrated into the community and succeeded in her program's growing goals. Not giving up and leaning into this experience turned out to be a time of exponential growth. It led to a deep love of sustainability and conservation that has blossomed into her life's work.

Susan has gone on to build a fruitful and meaningful career as a conservationist, documentarian, and filmmaker. In 1992, Susan wrote the pioneering book *Green at Work: Finding a Business Career That Works for the Environment,* and today is a member of the Film Committee for The Museum of Modern Art. Her award-winning films—*Mission of Mermaids*, *Food for Thought*, *Striking a Chord*, *Food for Life*, and *Making the Crooked Straight*—have aired on HBO, The Discovery Channel, and PBS. Her latest endeavor, *Musings*, is an online magazine that curates innovations and ideas centered around creating a more sustainable future.

Most things worth having require hard work. Challenging experiences can push you to gain invaluable perspective. Let the new experiences sink in. The journeys we find ourselves on are not always easy, but they will lead us to the future that is meant to be ours.

"People reinvent themselves
in every decade and you never
know where your life can take you.
The number one thing you can work
on within your control is how you
see the world and its opportunities.
Your positive energy will carry
you through and make you a star
in whatever you decide to do."

MEGHAN ASHA

Founder and CEO of FounderMade

MEGHAN'S FATHER, an Indian immigrant, came to the United States with nothing but a backpack and worked hard to become a successful entrepreneur. From an early age, Meghan felt pressure to push the boundaries of her own success, and her perfectionism led to some very difficult times. In college, Meghan struggled with an eating disorder and when it came time to enter the job market, she took a safe-bet position in finance. She was in a cycle of trying to please others and meet her own impossibly high standards.

While working in finance, Meghan found herself at a crossroads. She wasn't living in her truth and honoring her entrepreneurial spirit. So, when a friend encouraged her to attend a tech trade show in Las Vegas, she said yes. She quit her job and boarded a plane. If she hadn't said yes in that moment, Meghan may never have experienced the spark that ignited the idea behind her company. FounderMade started as simple dinners that brought entrepreneurs together to discuss their journeys and support each other and has grown to host the world's best retail conferences for the most innovative consumer brands in beauty, food, and wellness. Meghan is breathing new life and optimism into retail by connecting companies to buyers, consumers, and mentors.

When you feel like something isn't right, trust your gut. Trust that there are opportunities on the horizon that are more aligned with your soul's purpose and say yes to the new.

LIVE
FEAR
LESSLY

Don't let the fear of trying be greater than your fear of regret.

Beyond the obvious and tangible fears we all have, there are some fears that I refer to as "untruths," which are rooted in anxiety of outcomes that haven't even happened yet. These anxiety gremlins can paralyze us from exploring what could lead to our life's greatest adventures. Fears might include judgment from others, disappointing your parents, getting your heart crushed, or being vulnerable. Overthinking, assuming the worst, and living in fear can prevent you from taking a step in any direction.

———— • ————

It's easier said than done to shut off this noise within and be fearless. There is no one-size-fits-all method or advice for facing your fears head-on. Your own answer will come to you naturally when you do the inner work of assessing these fears.

The things we are most fearful of are often exactly the things we need to do to reach our greatest potential. My mom thought I was crazy when I first told her I was ditching my graduate school plans of becoming a psychologist to become a jewelry entrepreneur. Though I was fierce in my own belief in myself and the vision I had, there were plenty of fears that arose—fear of disappointing my mom, who had sacrificed so much and worked so hard to give me the life I had; fear of embarrassment if my business flopped; fear of how others would judge me; fear that I wouldn't make it.

Having clarity on what I was working toward helped me cast these fears aside and have a laser-beam focus on what I needed to do. I also knew that I would live with regret for the rest of my life if I didn't give myself the chance to just *try* and see what could become of it. Ask yourself, "Is my fear of regret greater than my fear of trying at all?"

Having a game plan and a fallback in place to combat your fears will push you forward despite the obstacles you'll face. In learning to face my fears head-on, I've grown, and so has my business. I've learned to say "yes" when opportunities present themselves, which has led to some of my most rewarding moments.

I realized much of my fear was rooted in my own lack of self-worth and confidence. We all have insights and experiences to share that can help others, and when we focus on the importance of the message we bring to the world and our greater purpose, those fear gremlins go away.

You'll be amazed at what starts to come to fruition as you shut out the noise within and become more fearless and focused. Feel that fear, then do it anyway.

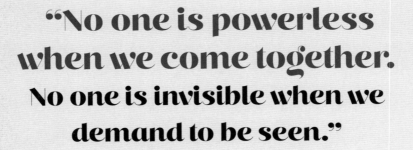

"No one is powerless when we come together. No one is invisible when we demand to be seen."

AMANDA NGUYEN

Civil Rights Activist, CEO and Founder of Rise,
Nobel Peace Prize Nominee

AMANDA'S FIRST LOVE was space and astrophysics. She attended Harvard University to further her pursuit of one day going into space. She excelled academically but in her final semester, Amanda was raped. In doing research about her rights, Amanda found that the laws surrounding the protection of sexual assault survivors were not uniform across the country and, in some cases, were downright horrific.

Amanda decided she would work to change the law and founded Rise, a civil rights nonprofit that trains and funds citizens to write bills and pass them into law. Amanda worked tirelessly to create a bill that would help sexual assault survivors and bring it to Congress for a vote. In 2016, the Sexual Assault Survivors' Bill of Rights was passed. It is the first wide-sweeping law that protects the rights of survivors across the United States. Rise has now worked to pass thirty-two more laws. And Amanda is taking her fight to the world stage. She is spearheading the first ever UN Resolution that would solidify survivors' rights as fundamental human rights worldwide. She was appointed by President Barack Obama to the U.S. Department of State as his Deputy White House Liaison and was nominated for a 2019 Nobel Peace Prize.

For Amanda, living fearlessly isn't about living without fear; it's about being cognizant of that fear and still marching on. It's okay to be scared, but know that you are fighting the good fight.

"The best way to move through fear is not by planning every single thing that could go wrong, it's by just **engaging with the world.** Just doing it, even when you have no idea what you're doing."

JESSICA EKSTROM

Entrepreneur and Author, Founder of Headbands of Hope

AFTER INTERNING AT a wish-granting organization one summer in college, Jessica started noticing that children battling illness often loved wearing beautiful, colorful headbands to boost their confidence when dealing with hair loss. She started Headbands of Hope with the mission to donate headbands to children struggling with illness.

Running a business, however, wasn't always sunshine and roses for Jess. In fact, early on, she wired a large amount of money to what turned out to be a fraudulent manufacturer. The money was a loan from a family member for the start of Jess's businesses and, unfortunately, she never saw it again. But Jess didn't let the fear of what might happen stop her from continuing her mission to do good. Headbands of Hope is now featured in thousands of stores across the world and has donated headbands to every children's hospital in America and fifteen countries around the world. Jess has gone on to write *Chasing the Bright Side* and is a motivational speaker, helping inspire other women to be fearless in their dreams.

Have a clear mission, and go for it. Know that there will be hiccups along the way, but that's all part of the process of learning how to be better and do better. Don't let your fear make you feel small. Use its energy to propel you forward.

"**All we have is now**
and the past is in the rearview
mirror—the future is not guaranteed.
Be in a place of ease with the unknown.
When you become at peace with the
unknown, you can really rest and relax
into the possibility of what you
want and can do."

MIKI AGRAWAL

*Social Entrepreneur and Author,
Founder of WILD, THINX, and TUSHY*

MIKI ISN'T JUST A SUCCESSFUL serial entrepreneur, she's an innovative disruptor. She is the founder of the restaurant WILD and innovative companies such as THINX (a company that makes patented period absorbing underwear and feminine hygiene products), and TUSHY (a company that makes modern bidets). Miki has found a space in the market for brands that think outside the box and disrupt the status quo. Miki is fearless in tackling taboo markets and talking about all things human. She is the author of *Disrupt-Her* and explains that we have to give ourselves permission to disrupt the illusions and limiting beliefs that stand in our way—that we can invent a whole new possibility for ourselves at any moment.

If you believe in your ideas, there will be others who do too. A valuable lesson Miki learned about business is the power of slowing down and taking a breath. Being at ease with the unknown meant she wasn't so worried about having the right answer in the moment or making the right decision as quickly as possible. That ease gave Miki the freedom to move forward fearlessly in her pursuits.

Being a disruptor means living fearlessly in your creativity. If you're fearless in your pursuit, people will gravitate toward you. That magnetism will manifest what you desire if you lead with love and live in the moment.

KEEP
AIMING

Our failures are our greatest teachers.

Our rejections and failures can be our biggest teachers if we choose to reframe them that way. There is always a lesson to be learned that was meant to prepare you for the next stage. You can let these moments defeat or fuel you; the choice is within your power. Think about some of the stories that have personally inspired you the most. Are they only stories of success, or are the stories of failure equally if not more inspiring? Learning how others overcame adversity—low points, hardships, heartbreaks, mistakes, and loss—and got to where they are today are what inspire me the most.

———— • ————

From designs that flopped, trunk shows with little to no sales, stores that told us "no"—I've dealt with endless moments that felt like failures in my decade in business. I've had many would've, could've, should've moments to reflect back on. But for every rejection and every "failure," there were five times as many successes. If at any point I chose to give up instead of learn from those experiences and push forward, I wouldn't be where I am today.

We are living in a time where we are overexposed to and overstimulated by social media. As inspiring and incredible as it can be to see into the lives of others, and the connections and opportunities these outlets bestow, it's also leading to comparison anxiety and constant feelings that we're not doing enough, we don't have enough, or we're falling behind.

Instead of saying "I wish that was me", allow other people's success to serve as an example of what you can achieve too. No matter what stage you're in, you'll always feel like you're not where you want to be if you compare yourself to others. It robs you of the joy and appreciation for how far you've come. We all deserve to be proud of ourselves, no matter where we are in our journey. There will always be a learning curve in anything you choose to pursue, and it takes making mistakes to advance to the next level.

To keep aiming is to pivot when something isn't working, to be adaptable, to try again, to keep aiming. It's the getting back up no matter how many times you've been knocked down—that's what's inspiring. I promise you, one day you'll look back at your "rejections" and "failures" and be grateful those things didn't work out because you ended up exactly where you needed to be.

When you keep aiming, you'll always be proud of your grit and determination. Look back at how far you've already come, and trust that your journey is only beginning.

"Get fired at least once in your life. It's important to know what that feels like—and it's really important that you hear 'no' at some point in your life, even for something that you truly want, because for every 'no' that means you have to look harder for a 'yes'."

STACY LONDON

Stylist, Author, and Former Cohost of What Not to Wear

A BUSINESSWOMAN, an author, a spokesperson, a stylist to the stars, and a television personality in her own right, Stacy has built her brand as a fashionista force to be reckoned with. Her rise in the fashion and media world, however, was not always linear. Getting fired from a senior fashion editor job at *Mademoiselle* magazine when she was thirty was a major turning point for her. While this rejection felt soul-crushing at the time, it led her down a much more rewarding path as a freelance stylist and ultimately cohosting the hit TLC reality makeover show *What Not to Wear*, which ran for ten seasons.

After reflecting on her career, Stacy has found that success and failure are both important stepping-stones on her journey through life. It takes courage to try new things and keep aiming to accomplish new goals. If everything worked out exactly as planned, we wouldn't hone the skills to adapt and take on challenges with excitement.

When you trip up, keep going, keep learning, keep aiming for your highest goals. Finding joy in finding your way will give you more fulfillment than a straight line to success. Your process is your own. That process can be messy. Find beauty in the mess. Your imperfect path is perfect for you. It will teach you the lessons you need to learn on your way to becoming the person you are striving to be.

"**Don't quit.
It implies you've already
started—which most of us have
in some way, even if our ideas are
still just daydreams. But the truth
is simple; if you don't quit,
you will succeed.**"

ELIZA BLANK

Founder and CEO of The Sill

FRESH OUT OF FINISHING her college education in communications at NYU, Eliza found herself looking for a passion that would lead to meaningful work. Then Eliza had moved into a six-floor, walk-up studio apartment on her own. Like many New York City apartments, it was a shoebox and lacked a personal touch and natural light. Inspired by her mother's green thumb, Eliza began to intentionally fill her small space with beautiful plants and greenery. The positive effect plants had on her life, along with her experience in branding, led to her light-bulb moment: plants were deserving of a consumer brand too! And thus, The Sill, a direct-to-consumer shop for the modern plant lover, was born.

Eliza started The Sill with a cofounder, but soon realized they weren't the right fit and parted ways after just a few months. Eliza continued on as the solo founder, which was one of the hardest things she's gone through, but also one of her biggest catalysts for growth and clarity. This "setback" brought her a newfound resiliency to handle challenges, which has gotten her through the countless others she's had to face.

When things don't work out—whether a business partnership, a job interview, or a failed relationship—rather than beating yourself up, look for the ways the experience built your resiliency. Find the lessons to be learned, pick that arrow up, and aim again.

"It took several years and starting my own company to realize that the only person standing in my way of achieving my dreams was me. You don't need specific diplomas or fancy endorsements to prove your worth. **The grit, the passion, the resilience ultimately come from within.**"

CAMERON ARMSTRONG

Founder and CEO of Kitty and Vibe

"KIND IS MY VIBE" is the slogan for Cameron's company Kitty and Vibe, a swimwear brand with revolutionary size inclusivity, as well as her personal check-in affirmation.

After moving to New York City from North Carolina following college, Cameron found herself struggling with anxiety. She was far away from what she had grown accustomed to, felt intimidated by her new corporate job, and was dealing with the difficult transition from student to working adult. With the help of therapy and acknowledging her mental health struggle, Cameron was able to build herself back up and become the strong woman, founder, and CEO that she is today.

Believe it or not, Cameron applied and was not accepted to business school, twice. She held a lot of embarrassment and resentment around this rejection for years, but pivoting toward her entrepreneurial pursuit with Kitty and Vibe allowed her to realize her own worth. Kitty and Vibe has gone on to become not only a successful business, but also a brand spreading positivity by building women up and encouraging them to embrace themselves.

It's easy to let the validation of the outside world direct our aim in life. Don't let bumps in the road define you. Next time you're feeling down, think, "Kind is my vibe." Be kind to yourself and be kind to others. If you keep your aim on the things you believe in, you may find yourself in an even better position than you could have ever imagined.

EMB
RACE
CHANGE

Trust the magic of change and new beginnings.

Our lives are made up of endless moments of change. Some of these moments of change are monumental, like choosing where to set down roots, and some are as small as changing your daily routine, but all of them affect where our lives take us. Sometimes the pain of nostalgia, or the fear of what lies ahead, can keep us from embracing the magic that change can bring. Each chapter of our lives will bring new challenges and growth opportunities. It's up to us whether we let our doubts stagnate us or embrace the change with open arms.

My mother emigrated to the United States from China at the age of thirty-five, leaving behind her career as an anesthesiologist in Beijing, and an unhappy marriage, to pursue her dreams of a new life. Even with a prestigious career as a doctor, the social structure limited what she was capable of accomplishing, and she felt that if she stayed she wouldn't have been able to accomplish everything she dreamed about. Having to start from the bottom up all over again, she was faced with some of the darkest times of her life.

She entered a new marriage filled with instability and hardship, dealt with language barriers and culture shock, and was isolated from everyone she knew and loved. Her life had changed in every way. Rather than give up, she kept full speed ahead and built a new life for herself that would ultimately be more fulfilling.

My mother is living proof that there's never a wrong time to make a change in your life. Every day, every choice we make determines our future, whether we realize it or not. Through each decade of your life, things will change and *you will change*—nothing is permanent.

The older and wiser you get, the more your inner beauty and appreciation will grow. You evolve into who you are meant to be, and every change, every experience you have, sews together the fabric of your life. You are never *stuck* and your past does not have to define who you *become*. We have more power than we realize to change ourselves and our circumstances.

Don't get caught up in timelines and pressures. Most success stories are decades in the making and filled with endless pivoting, rejection, and challenges along the way. What is meant for you will come when the timing is right. Some change we have no control over, and it's up to us how we frame it.

Extraordinary things can happen in the space between who you are and who you are becoming. Embrace change, because in this crazy, ever-evolving life, we could all do with a little more magic.

"I wish someone had told me to harness my stress and fear of change and turn it into motivation rather than let it slow me down. I wouldn't have wasted years worrying about careers and 'paths'."

NATASHA HUANG SMITH

Cofounder of Connectors and Creators,
Contributor to Harper's Bazaar

GROWING UP, NATASHA'S mother encouraged her to go into a well-respected, high-earning field like medicine. Natasha thought sports medicine would fit the bill. She worked with the NBA for a couple of years, but her heart just wasn't in it. Natasha needed a change, so she shifted into finance. She had a good thing going for a few years but ultimately burned out quickly. One day, she had an epiphany: "What would happen if I just did whatever I wanted and didn't follow a 'path'?"

Natasha ended a long-term relationship, packed up two suitcases, and bought a one-way ticket to New York with nothing but dreams and a scrappy mentality. She landed a job as an assistant at a national fashion magazine, and for the first time, felt really and truly alive. She had zero experience in the fashion industry and no money in her bank account, but she hustled and worked some of the biggest shows at New York Fashion Week. Eventually, she started her own boutique P.R. agency. One of the friends she made along the way, Morgan, became her business partner in her current endeavor, Connectors and Creators, a digital marketing and content business.

For Natasha, embracing change has become a lifestyle and she has learned to use change to her advantage. Let the spark of change excite you. Let the unknown keep you feeling alive. The next time a curveball is thrown your way, lean into it and knock it out of the park.

"The feeling of change

is all-encompassing. Try to embrace it instead of fear it! It's exciting to feel that these decisions and moments in your life can really shape your future, and when you look back on them you will remember the confidence you felt facing them."

KELSIE HAYES

Founder and CEO of POPUP FLORIST

WHEN KELSIE WAS in college studying fashion, she worked as a fashion stylist at a store called Beckley. After graduation, she moved to New York City to intern for a fashion designer. Despite this big move, Kelsie always made sure to maintain her relationship with Melissa Akkaway, the owner of Beckley, and it ended up being an important catalyst for Kelsie's career. She went on to work as a lead designer for Beckley for five years. It was a dream come true, but ultimately the brand came to an end in 2015.

Kelsie found herself questioning what step to take next. She was sensing a shift in fashion. Eventually, one night, after months of soul searching, an idea popped up in Kelsie's head: POPUP FLORIST. She had always enjoyed doing arrangements for pleasure, work, and friends; why not turn it into a business? Starting as just a Valentine's Day pop-up in a local coffee shop, POPUP FLORIST has turned into a fashion-forward, modern floral design company with a storefront, events, and e-commerce business.

Sometimes in life we're challenged to pivot. You can be full steam ahead in your chosen career and come to a sudden halt. This is where our ability to adapt, our support systems, and our imagination come in. Embrace change as an opportunity for growth. You never know who might come back into your life, offer a life-changing opportunity, or become a key support system in your pursuits.

"If you're not uncomfortable, you're not being challenged enough. This feeling will keep happening throughout your entire life because you're meant to move forward and escalate to new places."

DANA POLLACK

Founder and CEO of Dana's Bakery

DANA HAD GONE to school to study photography and had been working as a photo editor and event producer for over ten years. Her job at *Muscle & Fitness* magazine was fun, but she was working crazy hours and didn't feel fulfilled. She felt that if she didn't make a switch then, it would never happen. She had always loved baking for friends and family, and it brought her a lot of joy. So, within the span of one month, Dana quit her job, enrolled in culinary school, and broke up with her boyfriend.

Dana spent the following years attending school all day at Institute of Culinary Education, working at a restaurant at night, and developing recipes out of a commercial kitchen in her free time. During this time, she found an affinity for the French macaron, which became the staple of Dana's Bakery and propelled Dana into culinary success. Part of the reason for her success was the way Dana photographed them. She used her background in photography to elevate her new career in baking.

Accepting change can be difficult because it is inherently uncomfortable. But if Dana had not taken that big leap, she wouldn't be experiencing the fulfillment she does today. In the month that she threw caution to the wind, she found her passion and met the man who would become her husband. It gave her the push to ask herself, "If not now, when?"

TRAIL
BLAZER

Light the trail to your wildest dreams.

What defines a trailblazer, to me, is someone with a focused purpose, the unequivocal ability to pursue that purpose even when obstacles appear, and the desire to make sure that those who follow have an easier time. Being a trailblazer is success beyond material affirmation and financial gain. It's about forging a new path into a better world and pulling along as many people as you can in the process. Trailblazers push the conversation toward deeper compassion and acceptance. They challenge people to do better and think bigger.

———————————— • ————————————

A unique aspect of the trailblazer path is the level of pushback most receive early on in their journey. When you are the first to take a step in a new direction, you'll hit more friction because you are walking a path that hasn't yet been paved.

A trailblazer pushes beyond the initial difficulties because they believe in the importance of their mission. I think of women like Alexandria Ocasio-Cortez, stepping in as the youngest woman to ever serve in the U.S. Congress and spearheading modern legislature. I think of the people who fought for women's right to vote, who led women like AOC to where they are today. Trailblazers break free from the past and form the future. They are visionaries who don't let their circumstances define or limit them.

Now, you might be feeling intimidated thinking about all of the people that you regard as trailblazers. It's important to remember that these people who we think of as change-makers or pioneers started on a small scale. You have the ability to blaze your own trail starting now. Maybe it's standing up for yourself when someone is putting you down, or maybe it's volunteering to do charity work for a cause you are passionate about; big changes start with small steps.

No one woke up at the peak of their career and no one accomplished anything without overcoming some level of adversity. You might be ridiculed or looked at sideways at first, but if you push past this and believe in your principles and aspirations, life on the other side will be that much sweeter. When you are true to yourself, you inspire others to move forward with a greater level of authenticity. The world is a more interesting and beautiful place when we embrace our individual purpose and blaze a trail for a better future.

As Vice President Kamala Harris said in her election victory speech, "While I may be the first woman in this office, I will not be the last... Dream with ambition, lead with conviction, and see yourselves in a way others may not, simply because they have never seen it before."

"Being a trailblazer means paving the way for others.

My advice is to always be yourself, and stand up for yourself and what you believe in. Surround yourself with positive and supportive people who encourage you to follow and achieve your dreams, no matter what."

AMANDA LEPORE

Transgender Model, Celebutante, Singer, and Performance Artist

AMANDA HAS LIVED a life true to herself from the very beginning. As a model, artist, muse, socialite, and transgender icon, she is undeniably a trailblazer. Growing up in a household with a father who was not always accepting and a mother battling schizophrenia, Amanda experienced a tumultuous childhood. One thing, however, was always clear; she knew that she was a girl.

Amanda received a lot of pushback for just being who she was, but she didn't let that stop her from living the life she was meant to lead. She has moved the needle toward more transgender acceptance and, as one of the most marginalized communities, this is truly lifesaving. Amanda has written a memoir, *Doll Parts*, served consistently as the muse for famed photographer David LaChapelle, released a solo album titled *I . . . Amanda Lepore*, has graced the cover of multiple magazines, and continues to inspire the world with her authentic self.

If you feel like you're being judged for who you are, find a support system of people who love you, for you. A trailblazer is someone who sees themself clearly and doesn't let anyone dampen or deny that. Don't let anyone tell you that you are supposed to be anything but exactly who you are. Amanda has blazed the trail for so many who have followed in her footsteps, and has created a more accepting culture that will continue to expand for generations to come.

"As a musician,
I had to fight as a guitarist,
and as a guitarist in what
was a male-dominated field,
I had to fight as a woman.
These challenges motivated me
to work harder and become the best
player I could be. I've always viewed
adversity as an inspiration to
improve my skills and break
down glass ceilings."

SHARON ISBIN

*Grammy Award–winning Classical Guitarist
and Founding Director of the Guitar Department at The Juilliard School*

GROWING UP WITH two older brothers, Sharon was determined from an early age to break down gender stereotypes. She refused to allow anyone to limit what her interests should be just because she was a girl. As a teenager, she loved exploring the world of science. But, at age fourteen, after winning a classical guitar competition whose prize was to perform with the Minnesota Orchestra in front of ten thousand people, Sharon shifted her focus to music. She practiced for five hours a day, took summer classes at music festivals, and sought the best mentors she could find, including Dr. Rosalyn Tureck, one of the world's greatest Baroque music specialists and keyboard artists with whom she studied under for ten years.

Sharon is now a multiple Grammy Award–winning musician and one of the most acclaimed guitarists in the world. She was named the Musical America Worldwide Instrumentalist of the Year in 2020, hailing as the first guitarist to ever receive the honor in the fifty-nine-year history of the award.

Challenge the status quo and create your own space to thrive. Don't let labels define how far you can go. If your dreams are something that have never been done before, use that as an opportunity to be the first. But not just the first and only—the first of many. Because a trailblazer forges a path for themselves and all who follow. Show the world what you're made of.

"If you stand for something, it's quite possible you might be standing alone. That doesn't mean what you're standing for is wrong; you might just be the first one to speak up. That's totally okay, and people might think you're strange. Believe in yourself, have conviction, and **know that what you're doing is important.**"

LAUREN SINGER

Environmental Activist, Founder and CEO of Package Free Shop, and Founder of Trash is for Tossers

LAUREN ALWAYS HAD a strong inclination to help others, but it wasn't until Lauren read *Silent Spring*, by Rachel Carson, that her desire to help others shifted to the environment. She was upset by the negative impact humans have on the world just by virtue of unsustainable and unthoughtful choices. This inspired her to study environmental science at NYU and, in 2012, Lauren committed to living a zero-waste lifestyle.

Lauren went viral for fitting a year's worth of trash into a 16-ounce mason jar, but her impact on the sustainability movement has reached far beyond being "the girl with the trash jar." Lauren founded *Trash is for Tossers*, an online community that offers resources for living a more sustainable lifestyle. She has since launched Package Free, an online marketplace that elevates access to brands and products that are committed to reducing trash and environmental impact. Lauren's mission is to make sustainable alternatives to everyday products more accessible to the consumer.

At first, people told her that her zero-waste habits, from composting to making her own toothpaste, were "weird," but Lauren didn't let this keep her from living the true expression of her beliefs, and she continued to lead by example. To be a trailblazer means to not step down from your beliefs, even when the path ahead is clouded with judgment or doubt. When you blaze a trail you believe in, you'll inspire others to follow.

MOVE MOUN TAINS

Set your heart on it and there will be no mountain you can't move.

Life gives us a series of mountains we have to climb. They're put on our path to test us, teach us, and strengthen our will. In the moment, these mountains seem insurmountable, like the most difficult thing you've ever faced. However, once you're able to get past that first mountain you'll often be able to look back and realize it was merely a hill compared to the mountains that lie ahead.

———— • ————

With each mountain we climb and conquer, we increase our threshold and ability to handle even harder climbs and more treacherous paths. We develop confidence in our ability to overcome. Most things in life worth having are hard won. The mountains we face strengthen our ability to dream and work toward something greater. For some people, moving mountains could mean anything from passing an exam, being the first in their family to graduate college, or pursuing their dreams with a negative balance in their checking account.

There was a point in time when exhibiting at a trade show felt like an insurmountable mountain to me—I was worried about the investment costs, having a poor display compared to more seasoned companies, and not opening any retail accounts. Breaking even with a few thousand dollars in sales felt like moving a mountain, but looking back as we've grown to selling with hundreds of stores nationwide, that initial mountain feels like a pebble.

Year after year as we grow, the goals get taller, those mountains feel harder to reach, but as we begin to climb and conquer them, we look back and realize each mountain serves the purpose of leading us to the next. The biggest points of transformation and growth occur on the journey of getting there.

The process of growing, changing, and accomplishing your goals can feel daunting at times. Especially when you're starting out, you might lack the confidence to overcome and move mountains in this world. You don't have the life experience to back you yet.

Look to mentors or people on a similar path that you admire. It's important to reach out for support when you are trying something new. Learn to embrace the scary, motivating, difficult, and, at times, downright ugly process of navigating what life throws at you. It will test you, but with each mountain you move, you'll be that much more prepared for the next. When there's a will, there is *always* a way to figure things out. The mountains will get taller, but you'll be ready for the challenge.

"It's not about
moving one mountain;
it's about moving a mountain range.
You're going to get over one and have
to set sights on another. Surround
yourself with people you want to join
in your journey. Build a community
that you want to hike with."

BECKY STRAW

Cofounder and CEO of The Adventure Project

AFTER TAKING AN OPPORTUNITY after college to travel to Romania and work as a volunteer at a group home for children rescued from orphanages, Becky saw the impact of poverty and the suffering of others with new eyes. She yearned to find ways to help people in the most effective way possible while also treating them with dignity and respect. Becky decided to attend graduate school to garner tools for her work to have a greater impact, studying international social welfare with a focus on social enterprise at Columbia University.

She went on to help launch Charity: Water, an organization that brings water to people in developing countries, and consulted for UNICEF's division of water, sanitation, and hygiene. In her time doing this work, Becky noticed the most common thing people would ask her for was a job. So, in 2010, Becky launched The Adventure Project, an organization focused on providing tools, education, and mentorship for people to specialize in a skill. Once they garner a skill for a specific job, that job will allow them to work and offer services in their community.

Becky doesn't see her work as moving a single mountain, but a mountain range. For each mountain she and her team conquer, there is another mountain ahead. Choosing the people she surrounds herself with wisely, and learning to get comfortable with being uncomfortable, have been her biggest touchstones in navigating her life and work.

"At The Breasties,
we truly believe that
mountains are only placed in
front of those who can move them.
We believe that even on your hardest
days, no matter how great of a
mountain is placed before you—
you will move it."

ALLIE BRUDNER

Cofounder of The Breasties

ALLIE HAD JUST turned twenty-eight years old. She was at the beginning stages of a thriving career, had just gotten married, and was about to go on the honeymoon of her dreams. But after a fateful call from her doctor, she suddenly found herself in the midst of treatment for triple negative breast cancer. She felt isolated and like an anomaly. In the hopes of finding women like her to connect with, Allie began building a community of young women who were dealing with the effects of a high-risk diagnosis.

Out of that necessity for connection and support The Breasties was born. She created a space for women like her to come together and offer support, company, and a shoulder to cry on. Our tallest mountains seem less immovable when we have the support of a sisterhood behind us. Allie is now in remission and continues to grow The Breasties community as a beacon of light for those going through dark times.

Sometimes the adversity we face in life seems insurmountable. When a mountain is in front of you, remember that there is land on the other side. Think of the joy you can spread and the good you can accomplish. Think of the abundance of possibilities that lie ahead. Ask for the support of your community when you need it. If we support and lift each other up, there is no mountain we cannot move.

"While we can't always
choose our circumstances, we can
always choose our actions and responses.
It is easy to feel broken over something that
happens to you. But if you can turn that around,
and use it as a stepping-stone of strength, one
that helps you crystallize and clarify your vision
and your voice, then it can become part of
what makes you stronger and propels you
courageously out into the world toward
your higher purpose."

AMY ZIFF

Founder and Executive Director of MADE SAFE

IN HER THIRTIES, Amy suffered a tragic loss after miscarrying a baby boy. In her search for preventive measures to keep the same thing from happening again, Amy made a life-changing discovery about her own health. She learned that she, her husband, and the three children they would go on to have carried a gene mutation called MTHFR, affecting about half of the population. People who carry MTHFR don't detoxify or process chemicals as well as people who don't have the gene mutation. Amy realized the combination of the gene mutation and the chemicals present in everyday products was leading to allergic reactions in her twin babies that weren't otherwise explainable.

In her research, Amy learned that there are over eighty thousand chemicals in use in the world, but most are not evaluated for health and safety prior to going to market. She used this information to move mountains for others and educate the masses about the true weight of their purchases by founding MADE SAFE, America's first nontoxic seal for products. MADE SAFE vets and certifies products that don't contain harmful chemicals and are safe for use.

Sometimes it's the unexpected turns your life takes, the twists down a path you hadn't chosen, that bring the greatest opportunities. For Amy, it was a devastating realization that pivoted her down a path to advocacy, action, and discovering her higher purpose. There's always a way to move a mountain when you take action for what you believe in.

RIDE THE WAVE

Though the
waves of life, at times,
make us feel like
we'll drown, they also
teach us how to swim,
and remind us that
we'll rise again.

Highs and lows are a natural part of life and success, and the waves we experience craft the rich, bold, monumental chapters in our story. Just when the waters of your life feel calm and stable, a storm will roll through with an overwhelming surge that you can't always predict or plan for. These waves will inevitably knock you down, but they'll also teach you how to swim, how to survive, and how to keep going. They teach you the resilience needed to stay afloat. Learning to ride these waves is one of our ultimate purposes in this life; it builds our character, it defines us, it makes us stronger.

———— • ————

The year 2020 was the year of learning to "ride the wave" for me. My year began with a book deal, a successful round of trade shows, hitting major financial company milestones, and moving into our first showroom space—only for the world to be hit with a global pandemic a few weeks later that would bring a wave of panic, fear, sadness, and uncertainty. It was a challenging year for us all.

We had to learn to live without hugging our loved ones, struggle with financial instability, deal with the anxiety of a world in distress, and adapt to an unpredictable future. It was the year I got engaged and the year my beloved stepfather suddenly passed away. It was the year of some of my happiest moments and others that left me drowning, gasping for air. Life can and *will* throw you a curveball or plot twist when you least expect it. Giving into flow, learning that waves will crash and dissipate, knock you down and lift you up, will help you find solace in the fickle nature of life.

The waves I faced in 2020 taught me how to pivot my business, to be resourceful, to be proud of how far I've come and celebrate those milestones. They brought a new level of gratitude and love for the people in my life. They created more connection and community than I had experienced before. They reminded me of how precious life is, to not take it for granted. It's difficult to look for a silver lining in a year difficult for so many, but this pain and hardship have connected us all in a way only the human experience can.

In this crazy, unexpected, beautiful life, there will be waves that test your physical and emotional strength beyond what you think you can handle—but there will be just as many waves that help you rise, that carry you through, that push you toward your purpose. It's our choice to sink or swim.

"**Challenges in life**
have shown me how delicate
our time on this Earth truly is,
and the beauty of it is that we all
have the choice of what to do
with our precious time."

LEA D'AURIOL

Founder of Oceanic Global

OCEANIC GLOBAL FOUNDER Lea d'Auriol learned to navigate turbulent seas earlier than most. She experienced profound loss when her younger brother passed when she was only fifteen years old and then unexpectedly lost her mother shortly thereafter. This period of prolonged loss opened her up to the delicate nature of our world and our presence on this planet. She knew that whatever she wanted to do with her life, she needed to not only find meaning in her work but also create sustenance to protect those around her from further loss and show them the joys of life.

At age twenty-five, Lea read an article about our human impact on the ocean that would precipitate her life's purpose. That night, Lea mapped out the beginning of Oceanic Global. Initially starting as a passion project, Oceanic Global is now a worldwide nonprofit aimed at raising awareness for issues that have a negative impact on the ocean and instituting positive change. Oftentimes, the moments of deep sadness in our lives can lead to life-changing perspective shifts. Loss can offer a new appreciation for the preciousness of time. The journey of life naturally ebbs and flows. We often need to not only learn to swim but also find lessons in the changing tides to find our center and stay peacefully afloat.

Live in the feelings that come up, but know that you will reach land again, and you will look back and cherish the journey it took to get there.

"**If you're heartbroken,**
try to let yourself feel the feelings,
but don't forget to put yourself back out
there. I always say the best time to date
is when you're heartbroken because you
are less likely to get attached. And if you're
feeling defeated, just let it pass,
because it always will!"

LINDSEY METSELAAR

Founder and Executive Producer of We Met at Acme *Podcast*

WE'VE ALL BEEN unlucky in love at some point. Perhaps you've been cheated on or met someone who could have been the right person, but it just wasn't the right time. Lindsey found herself being dumped out of the blue on her twenty-seventh birthday. This felt like a wake-up call. She realized that there was a lot she had yet to learn when it came to dating and matters of the heart, and if she was feeling this way, there must be others in her shoes feeling equally as lost. She wanted to normalize conversations about dating, sex, and relationships.

As opposed to wallowing in heartbreak, Lindsey decided to launch *We Met at Acme*, a sex and love podcast that has propelled her into full-fledged millennial dating guru status. *We Met at Acme* has created a community of millennials navigating the world of dating through all of its trials and tribulations.

Heartbreak can be one of the most disruptive waves we experience. When you open your heart up to someone, you expose yourself to potential hurt. In order to feel all of the joy, fun, and sexiness that love has to offer, you have to give in and ride the wave of the unknown. Maybe you won't end up exactly where you wanted to be, but trust that the experiences along the way will build a better you. When that right love comes along, you will have become the person ready and able to accept it.

"Often our greatest difficulties
in life become our superpowers.
I used to think I couldn't be an actor
because I didn't want to be the center
of attention. But being a quiet observer
has greatly served me as a storyteller.
Lean into what makes you different.
I've found that it always ends up being
what people connect with most."

ESSA O'SHEA

Actor

GROWING UP AN introverted child, Essa did not think a career in acting was an obvious choice. While she was the baby of a family with six children, she wasn't putting on shows or seeking the attention of others. She did, however, enjoy storytelling. She was an avid reader from an early age and wrote poetry and short stories. It wasn't until a required theater class in high school that her love of acting and performance was born.

At the age of seventeen, she moved to New York City to study acting and screenwriting at NYU Tisch School of the Arts. Ultimately, she had to leave after her freshman year due to financial constraints. Essa made the courageous move to Los Angeles and managed to find her way on her own terms. With just seven dollars to her name at the time, Essa booked her first theatrical audition and was whisked off to Europe to shoot *Harley and the Davidsons* for the Discovery Channel. She has gone on to star in indie darlings such as *We Used to Know Each Other*, *Re/collection*, and *Mercy*.

Riding the wave for Essa has meant accepting the ups and downs of a career in the arts without a safety net and learning to make things work even when circumstances are working against you. In times of sacrifice, embracing your individuality can fuel your purpose to keep going. No one else can be you but you.

HEART OF GOLD

Cultivate a kind heart, and your legacy will be golden.

There is nothing more fulfilling than giving. It's a different kind of fulfillment, one that awakens your soul and brings a shock wave of energy and positivity. Kindness creates a domino effect; its impact reaches far beyond what you can even imagine. Our words matter. The moments we cherish are the ones that make our hearts feel full—like making your sister laugh until she turns red in the face or sending your friend a surprise birthday gift from across the country.

———— • ————

No matter how busy life gets, or how many times you trip and fall, the only things you'll regret when you look back is time you spent worrying, time you didn't spend with loved ones, the things you didn't say or the things you did say that you wish you hadn't. Focus on the quality of your intentions, not the quantity of your achievements. How you treat others lays the foundation of your life.

One of my dear mentors, Jordan, has a heart of gold. We met in New York City eight years ago when I was at a crossroads with the business and feeling lost and unsure of myself. She stepped in as the big sister and mentor that I needed, and helped me overcome my own self-doubt and insecurities. Her act of kindness became the spark of magic that I needed to move forward. She saw in me what I couldn't yet see. We all just need someone to believe in us.

One of my biggest missions through my business and brand ambassador program has always been to have a positive impact on young women. Whether it's encouraging them to believe more in themselves, offering them support in pursuing their passions, or connecting them to a community of other women, offering mentorship and a big sister for those who need it is part of the framework of f.y.b jewelry. One of our brand ambassadors a few years ago sent me a message thanking me for believing in her and helping her find confidence in herself. I still have this message saved and often look back at it in moments of my own self-doubt.

The most beautiful legacy you can leave behind is your kindness and generosity. If you're feeling lost or craving to make a difference in the world, think of one small act you can do today to help someone in need or put a smile on someone's face.

If you act from a place of love, that love will come back to you. Never underestimate the power of a handwritten note or going the extra mile for others. Love begets love. Heart begets heart. Be a catalyst for positivity in the world.

"There's so much fulfillment
in showing kindness and paying
it forward. I do this not because I have
more but because I stand on the shoulders
of a long line of changemakers who decided
to make the world a better place.
By living a life of impact, I am
leaving footprints for others
to do the same."

ROBERTA ANNAN

*Founder and Managing Partner of Annan Capital Partners
and Cofounder of Impact Fund for African Creatives*

ROBERTA IS NOT ONLY a powerhouse businesswoman and investor extraordinaire, but she is also a philanthropic soul and the youngest African to be inducted into the African Leadership Hall of Fame. Having been involved in impact investing, philanthropy, and advocacy, Roberta cannot overstate the importance of giving back. To her, acting with kindness, generosity, and empathy has rewarded her with more wholeness and satisfaction than anything else.

Roberta has dedicated much of her work to creating business opportunities for women in Africa. One of Roberta's milestone moments was partnering with The Lotte Accra and Adonai Child Development Foundation and the African Fashion Foundation to launch the Kayayei Collaboration Collection, a project that places Kayayei, a highly marginalized and vulnerable group of female porters—many of whom come from rural communities, into the workforce of fashion brands in Ghana. The mission of this collection is to equip, empower, and support young women by offering them skills and training opportunities with some of the most talented names in the fashion and garment industry in West Africa.

Giving back will always remain an integral part of Roberta's mission in life. Her mother put a strong emphasis on the importance of helping others and showed Roberta and her siblings that you can always find a way to help, even when it seems impossible. When you lead with heart, the world around you will follow suit.

"Giving to relationships without expecting something in return has been the biggest multiplier of value in my life."

HEATHER HARTNETT

CEO and Founding Partner of Human Ventures

HEATHER GREW UP in a community that put an emphasis on holistic wellness for the mind and body. Because this community revolved around making the world a more peaceful place, she always hoped to have a positive impact. Her father, an entrepreneur, encouraged a viewpoint centered around overcoming challenges and solving problems.

Once Heather graduated college, she took an internship in day trading but found that it didn't fit into the day-to-day life she hoped to lead or the values she wanted to live by. Heather went on to work in venture capital, and this led to the spark that would become Human Ventures, which focuses on cutting-edge companies and young entrepreneurs looking to offer solutions to problems. By connecting inspiring founders to capital, a supportive network, and opportunities to grow their expertise, Human Ventures uplifts entrepreneurs to excel in their respective businesses. Heather sees the positive impact for-profit companies can have when they offer sustainable solutions. She believes that entrepreneurs are the future of philanthropy and investing in them can be a powerful tool for change.

Having heart in business is essential to Heather. One of the meaningful lessons she's learned is the importance of surrounding herself with good people and giving and supporting without expectation. When you keep people who are also givers in your circle, you lift each other up. In business and in life it's important to approach relationships with an open heart and an open mind.

"Take time to do
your self-care, love yourself,
and nourish yourself well.
Treat yourself and others
with kindness."

ADRIANA CARRIG

Founder and CEO of Little Words Project

ADRIANA'S MOTHER IS a Mexican immigrant who moved to the United States and taught herself English at age eighteen. Growing up, Adriana was inspired by her mother's sacrifice, work ethic, and strong belief in self. In grade school, she was heavily bullied, and unfortunately, this bullying continued into her adulthood. Adriana decided that she needed to do something to spread a message of positivity.

She founded her company, Little Words Project, with the mission of encouraging women to be kind to themselves and others. The company's bracelets are handcrafted with inspirational words meant to be worn for as long as you need and then passed on to someone else in need of a little inspiration. Little Words Project has created a community of "nice girls" to spread a message of inclusivity with the hopes of making all women feel more loved and less alone.

When you experience negativity from others, there's an instinct to close off, but if you lead with an open heart, even when you are hurting, it is one of the purest forms of strength. Sometimes the people lashing out at us are hurting too. For Adriana, an important part of spreading kindness is making time for self-care. We have to help ourselves before we can help others. So take that hot bath, practice meditation, write in your journal, or make a delicious meal. Nourish your body and soul properly and the rest will follow.

POWER
FUL

You are
more powerful
than you realize.
Tremendous inner
strength and uniqueness
lie inside of you;
all you have to do
is harness it.

What makes you "you"? Though this question seems simple, many people are not able to truly answer this. Most of us spend a good chunk of our lives trying to fit in, and along the way we can lose our sense of self. What defines your style, what are your personality quirks, how did your culture or family life shape you, what's something few know about you? The path to self-discovery and defining who we are can be a lifelong process. It begins with recognizing our unique gifts, talents, personalities, and perspectives and *owning* these qualities rather than dimming them.

— • —

We are all dynamic individuals made up of layers and layers from our upbringing and childhood, to experiences that shaped our worldview, to our personal style and aesthetic that evolves over time. Being your unapologetically authentic self and embracing your individuality is the most powerful thing you can do in a world that tells us what to look like, what to wear, what to be, and what to believe.

No one has ever experienced the world *exactly* as you have. When we begin to think deeply about who we are beneath the layers and labels, our power emerges.

Another facet of owning your power is reframing your shame and recognizing the things that make you question who you are and whether you're worthy. I carried a lot of shame throughout my life from my family's financial hardships. It took years for me to reframe my shame and be proud of who I am and where I came from. Had I not gone through hardship in my childhood, would I be as resourceful, appreciative, empathetic, and ambitious as I am today?

Hardship builds character and grit, it makes our life story more interesting, and it's something I'm now grateful to have experienced. I no longer let others' close-mindedness affect me. The things we go through become part of our identity and our unique perspective, and no one can ever take that away from us. When you reframe your shame, you also forgive yourself and others, and there is nothing more freeing and powerful than that.

Never underestimate the value you bring to the world. Allow yourself to be vulnerable, raw, and real and you'll be amazed at the powerful connections you make with others. Your power, your perspective, and your stories make up your uniqueness. Let it strike everything you touch like a bolt of lightning and allow yourself to be a force to be reckoned with.

"No matter how painful it may be, or how much rejection or discouragement you receive along the way, being vulnerable, honest, and telling the truth always wins."

EMILY WARREN

Grammy Award–winning Singer-Songwriter

EMILY GRAVITATED TOWARD songwriting and music from a young age. She performed regularly with her band Emily Warren and the Betters and experienced some success early on when one of their singles, "Not at All," was featured in the MTV series *Skins*. Emily went on to attend NYU Tisch School of the Arts' Clive Davis Institute of Recorded Music, during which she was offered a songwriting contract with Prescription Songs.

Many of the rooms she entered were filled mostly with men and many of the songs female artists were recording at the time were written exclusively by men. Emily felt she was constantly coming up against inappropriate lyrics and hypersexualized song content that still felt normalized at that time.

Not long after, Emily had a session with Caroline Ailin, another female songwriter, and they decided to write a raw, unfiltered song aimed at setting rules to help keep people from slipping back into unhealthy dynamics. The song, "New Rules," was recorded by Dua Lipa and tied the record for the longest run on the Pop Songs chart. Emily has gone on to write for artists like Shawn Mendes, The Chainsmokers, Khalid, and Charli XCX. She became a Grammy-nominated artist for Dua Lipa's "Don't Start Now" and has released her own solo debut album, *Quiet Your Mind*, to much acclaim. She has used her strong female voice to own her power.

"It makes me uncomfortable that in our society beauty is centered around physical attributes like blue eyes and blonde hair; because beauty is so much more than that. It's how you feel and how you present yourself to the world. Beauty is broad, it's found in the parts of you that make you unique. For a long time, I let these societal ideas keep me from feeling beautiful. Embracing my true self and **owning who I am is what ultimately allowed my company to thrive.**"

ROOSHY ROY

Founder and CEO of Aavrani

ROOSHY'S PARENTS EMIGRATED from India to Detroit, where both Rooshy and her brother were born and raised. Growing up, she was bullied and teased for the very things that made up the vibrancy of her Indian culture. This naturally led to Rooshy comparing herself to the beauty standards being set by others. She stepped away from her Indian roots in an attempt to feel less alone and fit in.

When Rooshy started her company, Aavrani, skincare inspired by India's ancient beauty rituals, the ethos of the brand was to help women channel their inner beauty. But Rooshy still felt a strain in the duality of her own beauty and she hired another person to act as the face of the brand because she thought that her beauty was more outwardly acceptable. Subsequently, Aavrani lacked the genuine feel that customers crave. When Rooshy recognized that this lack of authenticity was having a negative impact on her brand, she decided to embrace her multicultural background and what made her story special. Rooshy enlivened her company with this newfound confidence. Launching a rebrand that was true to her, she stepped in as the face and founder of the company and the authenticity of her story resonated with consumers and financiers alike.

Embracing who you are is a process, but it is one that is so worthwhile. You are beautiful, and when you recognize that, it will be undeniable to everyone else too.

"I hope that I can inspire people through my normalcy in that I don't have the Michael Phelps talent or the iconic swimmer body that people see at the Olympic Games. I'm a small-town girl from Rhode Island who had this crazy dream and worked really hard to make it happen."

ELIZABETH BEISEL

Two-time Olympic Medalist in Competition Swimming and U.S. Olympic Team Captain

WHEN ELIZABETH WAS just six years old, her mother decided to take her to see her favorite Olympic swimmer, Amanda Beard, at a swim clinic. From that moment on, she trained, she competed, and she ignored the naysayers. People told her that she was too small or that she lived in the wrong state to become a swimmer, but she kept going. She harnessed her inner power and didn't let being shorter than height standards for swimmers keep her from pursuing her dreams.

And, at age fifteen, Elizabeth found herself walking behind Amanda Beard, having just made the U.S. Olympic swim team. She went on to qualify and compete at three Olympic games, winning a bronze and silver medal, and has won seven medals at an array of other international competitions. Elizabeth has now signed on to work as a swimming ambassador for SPIRE Institute, where she teaches and mentors other swimmers honing their craft.

When you have big dreams, you may find yourself on the receiving end of much doubt and discouragement: "What are the odds?" "It will never happen." "Try something else." But it's important not to let other people's ideas keep you from focusing on your goal. Believing in your power and ability to succeed begins with you. Harness that unwavering belief and break free of the doubters holding you back.

HUSTLE

Have the courage to hustle for your dreams and hustle harder for what ignites your soul.

Hustling isn't just an action, it's a state of mind. It's that scrappy, can-do, whatever-it-takes attitude that only our deepest passions can engender. It's the way we approach problems and what we are willing to sacrifice for the solution. Launching my own business at the age of twenty was the ultimate test of my own ability to hustle.

My family wasn't composed of entrepreneurs or business owners to guide me, and I had to figure out a lot of the hard stuff on my own—from setting up an LLC and filing sales tax, to building a website, pricing my collections properly, and everything in between. Running a business teaches you that there is no task beneath you, which is a very humbling experience in itself. To truly hustle is to be willing to work your butt off, take risks that terrify you, and know when to set boundaries so you don't burn out.

Opening my first pop-up store brought out a new level of grit and determination I didn't even know I had in me. When you are driven by a big dream, a passion, and wanting to prove to yourself and to others that you can achieve something, you'll be shocked by what you're capable of.

If you're venturing into a new career or business, shut out the noise and the naysayers. Trust that you have the patience and perseverance to make it work. Build equity in yourself. Learn and educate yourself in as many different skill sets as you can to build confidence in your abilities and identify what your strengths are, it will pay off in the long run. Start now in taking that step to invest in yourself. You will never regret working hard at something that makes you proud and builds your future.

The next time you hit a wall, ask yourself how hard you are willing to work to bring your vision to life. Look at your time management and assess how you're spending it. Are you *truly* dedicating enough time to work towards your goals? If you're feeling overwhelmed, think of just a few actionable steps you can take and set reminders to focus on them at some point each day.

If your idea or passion is something that you can't ignore, if it gives you a surge of energy when you think about it, it will all be worth it. If you have a purpose, your hustle will determine whether that purpose becomes a reality. Go after it with the full force of your being.

"You most likely will be working on your side hustle on the evenings or weekends. You have to put in the work, and the more work and effort and exposure you give your side hustle, **the bigger of an opportunity you'll create for yourself.**"

ALI KRIEGSMAN

Entrepreneur, Author, Cofounder and COO of Bulletin

FOR AUTHOR AND BUSINESSWOMAN Ali, *How to Build a Goddamn Empire* is not just the title of her book, it's a well-earned depiction of the rise of her company, Bulletin. Her company is an online community and marketplace connecting premium brands with retailers who have been properly vetted and verified. Bulletin has changed the way brands and retailers connect, and in doing so, has secured an astounding seven million dollars in funding.

Bulletin's success, however, didn't just appear out of thin air. It took hustle, drive, and guts to build. After being offered a job at an asset management firm, Ali realized that she had tricked herself into pursuing a career path that didn't actually align with her strengths. Rather than move forward with the job, she decided to put her focus on figuring out what work piqued her interest and played to her skill set. She asked to meet with and shadow professionals working in different fields. This is something she encourages other young women to do.

When Ali started Bulletin, it was a side hustle. It was something she worked on nights and weekends. For her, learning to manage her time properly was a huge part of Bulletin ultimately becoming successful. The more work and energy you put into your hustle, the more room for success you create. Remember, everyone starts somewhere. You just have to keep trying, keep learning, and keep hustling to make your dreams a reality.

"Go day by day and do everything in your power to **work toward your goals.** I try to stay conscious of not letting overthinking fully paralyze me into never doing anything at all."

DANI EGNA

Founder and CEO of Inked by Dani

IT WAS ONE night in college. Dani and her friends were getting ready to attend a themed party. Dani, a fine arts major, was called upon to draw fake tattoos in eyeliner on everyone to add to their costumes. After unbelievable feedback about her body artwork throughout the night, she decided to enter the temporary tattoo industry.

When entering an untapped market, it's easy to doubt the validity of your idea. If it's never been done before, there's no way of knowing the outcome. For Dani, it was all about trusting her vision and hustling to make it become a reality. In order to scale up and meet the demand that she was receiving, Dani needed to relinquish control and hire employees so that she wasn't doing every step herself. As a perfectionist, Dani found this difficult, but delegating ultimately allowed her more time to focus on design and growing her business.

Hustle isn't all about just putting one foot in front of the other. Staying organized in your plans and knowing when to ask for help is an important foundation for growing your idea into a full-fledged success story. Having clear intentions of what to work on can help keep you from overthinking. When you have actionable steps, you're less likely to get lost in the shuffle of the hustle. The more thought and intention you put in ahead of time, the less likely you are to get lost along the way.

"Don't be afraid to take risks in your career. It's easy to stay in your comfort zone, but you will never truly grow until you learn to embrace change and at least try the opportunities that come your way. Stretch your skills as far as you can and always be willing **to listen and learn!**"

PARKER BOWIE LARSON

Style Director of ELLE Decor

FOR PARKER, LANDING the position of assistant market editor came with a mixture of emotions. Coming from the South, she was ecstatic to be moving to the Big Apple, but she soon realized that she had a lot to learn. One night, after completely dropping the ball at a photoshoot, Parker told her friend that she just didn't think she could do it. Her friend told her that all she had to do was make herself irreplaceable.

From then on, Parker pushed herself even harder and leaned into the hustle. She learned not to take "no" for an answer, and when things didn't work out the way she wanted, she found an alternative. She cultivated the skill of anticipation, always foreseeing two steps ahead what her boss might ask of her. Parker excelled in her career, growing from an editorial assistant role at *Cottage Living* magazine to market director at *Architectural Digest* to her role now as the style director at *ELLE Decor*.

The hustle is about pushing yourself past your own expectations of what you can accomplish. Rather than giving up when the going gets tough, figure out an alternative solution. When you're entering a new space, whether it's a new job, relationship, or phase of life, there's always a learning curve. Give yourself grace but challenge yourself to step up and meet the task at hand. With enough imagination, grit, and hustle, anything is within reach.

PERSE
VER
ANCE

To persevere is to commit with unwavering patience and desire to see your dreams through.

Perseverance is learning to transform the low moments into forward motion. It's fighting the urge to quit. It's believing in something bigger. The most beautiful things can come from the hardest of circumstances. You must grow through what you go through in your life to become the beautiful person you're meant to be.

———◆———

When I was a toddler, my parents and I lived in a spare bedroom of my uncle's house for a period of time. My father was making ends meet working for his cousin's construction company and after my mom's Exchange Visitor Visa scholarship ended at the hospital, she had a hard time finding employment. Her medical degree didn't translate here in the United States. As a means of survival, she started making dumplings and selling them to neighbors and friends of friends through my father.

My mom eventually landed a job as a live-in caretaker for a woman with Alzheimer's while staying up all hours of the night to study for her phlebotomist certification. This was exceptionally hard for her, as she was still learning English and had to translate every page with her Chinese/English dictionary. My mother passed the exam and went on to excel in her career, eventually becoming a cardiovascular technologist and the breadwinner of our household.

My mom imbued in me the importance of financial independence and defined what it truly takes to persevere. *Self-doubt* was not a word in her vocabulary; there was no luxury of "giving up." It was the fire within her, the hunger for more, to not accept reality as is, that gave her the strength to climb out of the darkest times.

To persevere is to commit—committing to yourself, to your dreams, to your vision, to your passion. When you commit to something, patience is key. Nothing is immediate, and there are no "overnight successes." Most people who we think burst onto the scene had careers that were a decade or more in the making and were told "no" endless times. This is especially important in the "Amazon culture" of today. We expect immediacy and for everything to happen *now*. When our careers, our great loves, or our financial successes don't come quickly, we feel like something is wrong. Not everything can be delivered to your doorstep in twenty-four hours.

It takes time to build something great. Perseverance is dedicating yourself to the long haul. Focus on why you are doing what you are doing and let that carry you when things get tough. If you do something long enough, if you truly commit, you will find success on any path you pursue. Let your passion pull you through the mud, and you'll always find your way.

"In the face of obstacle after obstacle, adversity, insecurity, and self-doubt—just showing up and giving what you have is enough in any given moment. No effort is wasted, even if you aren't sure how it will turn out. Never give up. **Because as long as you're in the game, there's still a chance you'll win.**"

TIANNA BARTOLETTA

Two-time Olympic Gold Medalist in Track and Field

TIANNA WON HER first world title as an American track and field athlete in 2005 at just nineteen years old. It would be ten years before she would win a world title again. In the time that elapsed after her first title, Tianna found herself constantly striving to get back to the form and mind-set that led her to a win. She was falling short in her goals. She was being called a "has-been" athlete who was just working her way out of her career. Her confidence was broken.

Tianna decided to develop a plan to use the money she was making as an athlete to fund the rest of her college education. But in order to do this, she still had to train and compete at a high level. So, she hired a new trainer and recommitted herself to the preparation required to be competitive. Four months after training six days a week, Tianna was lined up to compete in the 60-yard dash. Tianna not only won the race, but she also ran the world's fastest time.

Tianna went on to become a two-time Olympic athlete, winning three gold medals. If she had given up, listened to the commentators, or let the disappointment consume her, she wouldn't have experienced everything she had worked for coming to fruition. Perseverance is about doing the work, even when self-doubt arises. The days will add up and you may just find yourself on the brink of your wildest dreams.

"My expectation is not that I'm going to have to keep working or I will become obsolete. My expectation is that I am going to continue learning and pivoting and growing and changing until I feel satisfied. I never feel like there is a limit or anything finite to what I can do or be."

VERONICA WEBB

Model, Actor, Writer, and TV Personality

VERONICA IS A BONA FIDE supermodel. Although Veronica's success is undeniable, she recognizes the amount of work it took to reach these heights. The fashion industry is cutthroat as is, but Veronica was also setting new standards as the first African-American supermodel to have a major cosmetics contract.

Veronica has never been afraid to challenge the status quo for the betterment of the world. It takes perseverance to stand up and face adversity, and for Veronica, persevering became a way of life. When hair stylists would send her home because they didn't know how to do her hair, she kept going. When she heard that brands were not going to include her in their campaign because of the color of her skin, she kept going. When her age started to be perceived as a negative, she kept going. Instead of letting these experiences own her, she reinvented the game. Thirty years later, she has continued to walk in runway shows with brands including Yeezy and Sophie Theallet and is featured in international fashion magazines including *Vogue, WWD*, and *ELLE*.

Just because something hasn't been done before, doesn't mean it's not possible. The next time you feel like you can't do something or keep going, remember the women who came before you. Remember the work that you do isn't just for you, it's also for the women who will follow in your footsteps. Leave a legacy that is undeniable.

"Creative paths are always long, and it's very rare that young creatives find success quickly. You have to endure it, stick to it, and prevail. You will get there when you get there. Endurance and consistency are more important than talent. If you just stick to your job and do it enough— **one day you'll be great.**"

GABRIELA HEARST

Creative Director of Gabriela Hearst and Chloé

GROWING UP ON her family's ranch in Uruguay gave Gabriela a deep appreciation for practicality and sustainability. Everything her family used in their day-to-day life was homemade and therefore had a special quality and consistency to it. For thirty years, Gabriela's grandmother made the same cake recipe every week. Since then, other family members have tried to replicate it, but it's never tasted quite the same. This was Gabriela's first example of the power of perseverance. If you do something for that long, endurance and consistency become more important than talent. If you dedicate enough time to something, you will eventually become great.

This upbringing has become the foundation for Gabriela's brand, a fashion powerhouse focused on combining luxury with integrity and transparency, while putting an emphasis on sustainability. Many of the materials used in the creation of Gabriela's clothes come from the family ranch that she now runs, and she is committed to using biodegradable packaging and investing in zero-waste practices.

Perseverance is a journey that starts within. It's committing to yourself and working hard to see your dreams through. Honor the fundamentals of how you were raised and the people who have had an impact on your life. Let this foundation guide you in finding the ideals and principles that you want to live by. When an obstacle arises, know that your soul, deep down, has the courage to persevere. Hard-won accomplishments are that much sweeter.

U N
BREAK
ABLE

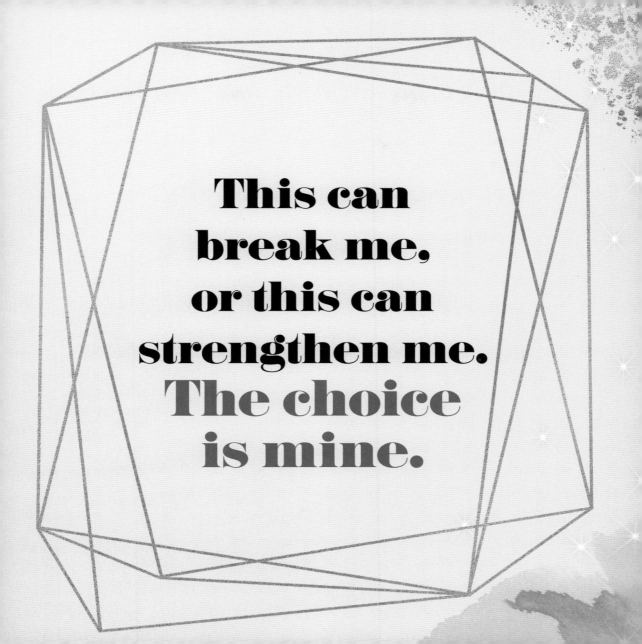

This can break me, or this can strengthen me. The choice is mine.

To be broken up with by the person you thought was the one, to have your heart broken from loss, to be utterly broke and worried about affording the simple necessities: these moments, of the bend before the break, test our limits, our desire to keep going, to wake up each day and face reality. Don't underestimate your power to overcome and take charge of whatever circumstances or hardships life throws at you. We all experience these moments of sadness or weakness, they strengthen us, soften us, and become core to who we are.

———— • ————

When you feel like you can't keep going, when you've hit rock bottom, remember that the only direction from there is up. Time will heal your wounds, your inner strength will guide you, and you will smile and laugh again. Understand that pain will come and go, but with patience, it will help you grow. Give in to the messy breakups, the bad days, the accidents, and mistakes—these are the experiences that will build your character. Know that you will be okay. Life only gives us what we are strong enough to handle.

In my own life, some of my most painful experiences taught me my greatest lessons. My father's struggle with undiagnosed bipolar disorder and the impact it had on my childhood taught me compassion, empathy, and forgiveness—and to realize our parents are humans too. My parents' divorce taught me to learn to let go of things that are outside of my control and instilled maturity in me at a young age.

My several heartbreaks each opened my eyes to new versions of love and taught me more about myself and what to look for in a partner. The pain of my stepfather's stage 4 colon cancer diagnosis and tragic passing taught me to never take a moment spent with loved ones for granted. Through all of this, I ultimately learned that our greatest heartaches can also bring gifts, we just have to be open to finding them.

It is often difficult to be hopeful when we're in our lowest, most painful moments, but don't underestimate the power you have to take charge of whatever circumstances or changes happen in your life. Maybe you won't be able to define the positive takeaways at that time, but you can almost always look back and find how an experience shaped you into the stronger person you are today.

To be unbreakable is not to harden, but to be resilient through the hardest times. To allow optimism to power you through the pain, to pick up the shattered pieces and find yourself again.

"Being able to talk to other people, whether you're close to them or not, who have gone through the same thing as you is just so freeing. **Focus on your healing,** be patient with yourself, and allow yourself to grieve when you need to."

SARAH LARSON LEVEY

Founder and CEO of Y7 Studio

AFTER JUST RETURNING from Los Angeles, where she was opening Y7 Studio's Silverlake location, Sarah received some devastating news. She had suffered a miscarriage. Her business was growing at a momentous rate, as they were preparing to open their new studio in Tribeca, with more locations on the horizon, but Sarah was crumbling inside. Unable to process the grief at the time, Sarah threw herself into work. Y7 continued to grow and it wasn't until Sarah's second miscarriage that she was able to take a step back and process the loss with her husband.

Sarah began reaching out to her friends, and the Y7 community, and found solace in being open and honest about her hardships. She found herself connecting with those who had had similar experiences. She gave herself the room to feel, and in turn began to heal. Knowing she wasn't alone and having a supportive community helped her find the strength to keep going.

Sometimes things happen that shatter us to pieces and make us feel like we will never be whole again. But nothing can break you if you keep moving forward. Process in your own time. Reach out to your community when you need support. Believe in your own strength to take on anything. Sarah and her husband have since been blessed with a son, and Y7 Studio continues to grow as an unyielding force in boutique fitness.

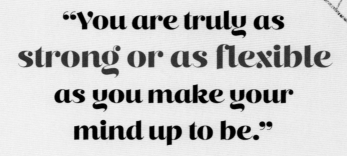

"You are truly as strong or as flexible as you make your mind up to be."

HEIDI KRISTOFFER

*Founder of CrossFlowX,
Creator and Producer of Microsoft Bing Fitness Yoga
and MSN Yoga*

AFTER A TERRIBLE car accident at eighteen left her with two broken vertebrae, multiple herniated discs, and a straightened cervical spine, Heidi found herself in and out of doctors' offices. She was told surgery was necessary. She was told she would need a steel rod in her spine. She was told she would never do yoga again.

Yoga to Heidi is not only a sacred personal practice but also her business. Heidi is the creator of the uber-successful CrossFlowX, the CrossFlow app, and producer and creator of MSN Yoga and Microsoft Bing Yoga. She has been on a mission to bring yoga to the masses and has created a conversation around wellness, green and clean living, and boss-hood with her podcast *Off the Gram*. Instead of letting the news from doctors break her, Heidi looked inward. She had the vision that with enough resilience, time, and attention, she could heal her body. She found and worked with doctors who believed in her process and, over time, her body healed without surgical intervention.

Don't let the weight of bad news break you down. Use opposition to fuel you through. There is never just one solution to every problem. If you have the courage to live by your convictions, you may end up making discoveries that help improve the world around you. Heidi proved that with enough care and belief, you can be unbreakable.

"Let me assure you that you can survive even the worst days and see the light again. Even when you experience the worst thing you can imagine, hope and happiness will find you. You survive and end up stronger than you were before."

JULIA BROGLIE

Founder and CEO of BroglieBox

THERE WAS A POINT in Julia's life when she felt completely shattered. She was dealing with the devastating heartbreak and finality of her brother Justin's suicide, and she couldn't help but feel like his death could have been prevented. Sometimes we can't help but blame ourselves when tragedy strikes. But ultimately, we can't change what has already happened. This reality can either leave us feeling hopeless or encourage us to find the strength to lead with hope.

Justin's passing inspired Julia to cofound BroglieBox in his honor, to help others who are dealing with mental health issues feel less alone. BroglieBox provides resources, actionable steps, and evidence-based tools for those struggling or looking to maintain their mental health. For Julia, the most important part of moving through grief was challenging herself to just keep going and picturing a time when things wouldn't feel so dark. Channeling her grief into meaningful work has given her purpose and offered a validating way to move forward.

When tragedy strikes, we can feel like nothing will ever be the same. The truth is, it won't. But light will shine in your life again. And when you pick up the broken pieces of the life you had, you will make a new mosaic: a picture full of the happy times, the great love, the deep pain, the unimaginable loss, and all of the other experiences that make us all beautifully and imperfectly human.

WING
WOMAN

If we are there
to lift each other up,
there are no obstacles
we can't soar through,
and no heights we
can't reach.

Our wing women are the ladies in our life who cheer us on and believe in us through both our brightest and our darkest moments. They are the ones who show up with a bottle of wine and a carton of ice cream when we're going through a breakup or a hard time at work. They listen to us vent and help us pick ourselves back up. They don't judge our decisions, are genuinely happy for our success, and understand and see us for who we are. What is success without having those we love to celebrate and share it with?

———— • ————

"If you want friends, you have to be a friend"—this is a sentiment my mom would share with me as a little girl and I have carried it with me into adulthood. If you're not feeling loved and supported, are *you being* loving and supportive? How you treat others will always come back to you. Changing your approach will change your relationships. As simple as this is, we often forget that relationships are not a one-way street.

We can't assume others know what we need. We all show love in different ways. Communicate with your people and when you feel a lack, show them support first. That support will come back your way and increase like a ripple effect, touching everyone in your life. I can't tell you how many times my friendships, connections, or network of women have guided me through.

It's not always easy to find your "tribe," especially at moments of transition: going away to college, moving to a new city, or starting a new job. There are endless ways to connect with like-minded women in all stages of your life, such as by joining a sorority or getting involved with women's networking groups in your area. It's important to put yourself out there and challenge yourself to step out of your comfort zone. It may feel weird in the moment, but it's the first step to making a connection.

There is nothing a woman with a supportive tribe of women beside her can't do. We are stronger together. When we adopt an attitude of collaboration over competition, when we realize others' success doesn't dampen our own, when we approach others with love and genuine connection—that's when we all truly thrive.

When these wing women come into your life, like magic beams of sunshine, hold on to them tight. Treasure them, support them, show up for them. You are who you surround yourself with; let that group be the most amazing, supportive, loving, understanding, group of women they can be.

"Always remember that you can **build your tribe anywhere!** You could meet your future business partner at a coffee shop, sitting on the subway, or at the next event you attend. Never be afraid to put yourself out there and be confident. Let your passion and authenticity shine through; it's sure to bring you far."

LISA MAYER

Founder and CEO of My Social Canvas

WHEN LISA STARTED My Social Canvas, it was just an accessories brand, but it has expanded into so much more. Her products are designed by girls, for girls. Through mentorship and practical real-world application, she is on a mission to help Gen Z girls and women design the career and life they love. Lisa has also created a community through My Social Canvas that offers a support system for young women navigating the ups and downs of entering adult life and entrepreneurship.

For Lisa, finding her tribe in New York has been a journey and not something that happened overnight. From serendipitous moments of starting conversations with people in line at a restaurant that led to influential connections to confidently introducing herself to new people at conferences and events—Lisa's approach to connecting with others is focusing on what she can give rather than what she can gain and building genuine friendships.

Two of her early mentors, Judy and Martha, who were working executives in their own right, have continued to be huge beacons of support. Now Lisa mentors Martha's daughters and the support network they have nurtured continues to grow.

Remember that even top CEOs get nervous about meeting new people. You never know who will be that life-changing connection, so put yourself out there and lead with confidence and love.

"Find women who **believe in you,** who will lift you up, who will be your cheerleaders, but most importantly, find women whose own passions galvanize you to invest in your own."

KATYA LIBIN

Cofounder and CEO of HeyMama

BORN OUT OF the necessity for working mothers to have a space to reach out for support, HeyMama connects and forms communities for women who are trying to navigate building a family while building a career.

For Katya, cofounder of HeyMama, the journey as an entrepreneur has been filled with euphoric highs and devastating lows. Navigating the demands and unknowns of motherhood and business simultaneously can feel daunting. Katya attributes much of her ability to cope to the balancing force of the strong women in her life. The women in her network, including Johanna Zeilstra, CEO of Gender Fair, Alison Wyatt of Female Founder Collective, and Stacey Heuser, president of the Narrative Group, have helped her synthesize business concepts, lifted her up when self-doubt was at its highest, opened doors that have been tantamount to the success of her business, and even helped her raise money for HeyMama.

Life, motherhood, and maintaining a healthy work-life balance are hard. Let your community lift you when you are low. Reach out when you have questions, need advice, or just need someone to talk to. Expand your circle and create a community of like-minded wing women who are advocating for each other. When you fall, your tribe will be there to catch you; and when you soar, they will be there to cheer you on.

"When I finally opened up
and started to lean into being vulnerable
and authentic online, it opened doors
to attract the community and connection
that I had been longing for forever. It made
me realize my passion for providing
visibility for female founders and providing
a platform to amplify their missions. To me,
there's just nothing better than women
coming together from a place of
genuine love and support."

LISA ROSADO

Founder and CEO of We Are Women Owned

GROWING UP, Lisa often felt disconnected from her family and community. She had two sisters, one who was significantly older and wasn't in the same phase of life, and a younger sister who struggled with a mental and physical disability. This engendered a feeling of loneliness. As an introverted kid, Lisa lacked some of the confidence to reach out to other girls her age. Additionally, she feared the catty and competitive nature that can be prevalent in female relationships. What she truly desired was a community of women who supported each other in the purest form—a group dedicated to respecting individuality and encouraging each other to fly.

In her time attending college and working for fashion boutiques, Lisa hadn't yet found the community that truly fit her needs, so she created it. Extending from the community she curated from her blog and online shop, The Style Theory Collective and building on her desire to give back, Lisa launched We Are Women Owned, or WAWO. WAWO is a membership community dedicated to supporting women-owned businesses through an online directory, events, networking, and promotion.

When women join forces and lift each other up, we become that much more powerful. We don't have to be competitive or constantly compare ourselves to each other. There is space for everyone. When you are confident in your individuality, and what you have to offer, you encourage others to feel the same. Reach out and share your passions. We're in this together.

THINK POSI TIVE

We become what we think about. Believe in the power of your own thoughts and manifest your destiny.

Positive thinking, vision boards, and gratitude greatly shaped the course of my life. Mind-set is everything. Our thoughts are more powerful than we realize. What we focus on expands and manifests itself. I made my first vision board when I was seventeen, clipping images of things that represented love and success to me. My vision boards have changed endlessly over the years as I've changed and grown. They have served as a spiritual road map that keeps me excited and focused when I feel off track, reminding me of where I'm heading and where I've been. The exercise of visually collecting your goals on paper awakens a different energy within you, because it makes your goals feel a little more concrete than fleeting ideas in your head.

If you make the effort to sit down and think about what you want and put it on paper, you're committing yourself on a higher level to achieving it. It's an amazing tool that helps you channel your energy and thoughts in a positive direction and is the perfect place to start if you're feeling lost.

An important element of manifesting your vision and embodying a positive mind-set is having gratitude. It's the secret sauce that amplifies everything and reminds you of what's most important and how much you already have. Alongside my vision boards, I create a gratitude board consisting of images of my family and friends, company milestones, screenshots of sweet notes from customers and brand ambassadors—things that remind me of how much I already have in my life and how much love I'm surrounded by.

To think positively is to focus our energy on the things that ignite excitement, gratitude, and love within us. It's to get still, shut out the noise, and let our inner voice guide us. It's allowing ourselves to pause and breathe, take a break from the constant "go, go, go" mentality, settle into the present moment, and change our attitude. It's a conscious choice we make when we wake up every day.

Optimism will get you so much farther in life than pessimism ever will. It's the ability to reframe any circumstance we're in to find the silver lining rather than focus on the dark cloud. It's not allowing ourselves to downward spiral in comparison, negative self-talk, or criticism. It's defining what personal fulfillment and success mean to *us*.

We can't allow ourselves to get so caught up in "arriving" that we fail to appreciate the journey of "getting there." With a positive mind-set, a grateful heart, and a clear focus, you can become a force to be reckoned with.

"I don't really believe in 'can't.' I think if you're passionate enough about something, you can manifest almost anything. Being positive is a lifelong pursuit that falls in line with always learning and growing."

LARISSA THOMSON

Cofounder of ONDA Beauty

WHILE WORKING AS a fashion market director, Larissa adopted yoga and self-care practices to give her life more balance. When she was starting to feel the desire to move on from magazines and fashion, Larissa had a light-bulb moment one night while she was researching beauty ingredients. Health and wellness was something she was passionate about, so why not create a space where that is the center of discussion? With the help of her cofounders, Sarah Bryden-Brown and Naomi Watts, Larissa founded ONDA Beauty, a holistic, clean beauty destination.

To Larissa, holistic beauty is a choice you make about how you want to live your life. It encompasses how you eat, sleep, and treat your body inside and out. When you honor your body and spirit, your output in the world will be exponentially better. The same is true of your thoughts. Larissa believes that if you are passionate about something, you can manifest almost anything. When she is unsure of what direction to take, she tries to listen to her body's natural response. If the thought of something makes you recoil, it is probably not in tune with your purpose. If something enlivens you, explore it.

Onda means "wave" or "flow." Think of it as the flow of energy in your life. You have the power to form that energy how you see fit. Own who you are. If you think positively, the glow will be seen for miles.

"Having a positive mind-set is your *choice*. When presented with adversity, there's an opportunity to expand the lens through which we're experiencing something so we can see beyond that moment. We can *choose* to see a future that isn't limited by one moment in time."

JANET MACGILLIVRAY, J.D, LL.M

Founder and Executive Director of Seeding Sovereignty, Lawyer

HAVING A POSITIVE outlook has been a driving force throughout Janet MacGillivray's life and career as a single mother, two-time breast cancer survivor, and lawyer. Janet left home at seventeen under challenging circumstances and made her way to New York City with just five duffel bags in tow. She took on multiple jobs, cleaned houses, and put herself through school eventually graduating from Columbia University and New York University with a Master's in Environmental Law.

She pursued a career in water law, defending violently oppressed communities whose water and forest systems are threatened by corporations. In 2016, she was invited to Standing Rock by Chief Arvol Looking Horse. While the historic fight at Standing Rock initially ended in what felt like a crushing defeat, it also had seeded a beautiful community and new leadership. Janet made a choice to imagine and build a container for true environmental stewardship for a more just world. This led her to launch Seeding Sovereignty, an Indigenous-led collective working to radicalize and disrupt colonized spaces through land, body, food sovereignty work, community building, and culture preservation.

For Janet, not always knowing the answers has led to her greatest moments of discovery and connection. By not always knowing the solutions, you invite others to speak and lead which helps us to learn from one another and build a circle that grows and inspires. Thinking positively sometimes means *trusting*—trusting others, trusting your choices, and trusting in what the future brings.

"If I could tell my twenty-five-year-old self one piece of advice, it would be comparison is the killer of joy. At that age, I was looking at everyone around me, saying, 'Why am I not as pretty as that person or as fit as that person?' or 'Why don't I have a job like that person?' At that age, you think you know what you want, but you're not sitting down and asking yourself what you actually want. Be clear on the difference between **happiness and true fulfillment.**"

MICHELLE CORDEIRO GRANT

Founder and CEO of Lively

MICHELLE GREW UP the daughter of immigrants in rural Pennsylvania. There was one Indian family in her town: hers. Her parents exemplified a strong sense of resilience and adaptability. This instilled a powerful personal identity in Michelle.

She moved to New York City, entered the world of fashion, and worked at Victoria's Secret for five years overseeing merchandising and strategy. While working there, she noticed that most women were uncomfortable in their undergarments. They were wearing the wrong size, the fabric was rough, or the straps pinched their skin. This inspired Michelle to launch Lively, a lingerie brand designed by women for women, as an answer to these issues.

Lively has become a game-changer in the lingerie market, but she often reflects on the time before her company took off. She lived with her husband in a 400-square-foot apartment. For Michelle, with the addition of success and resources, her happiness level hasn't changed from her time in their tiny apartment.

There is often a strong emphasis on material gain or business growth as a marker for personal success. It is important to Michelle that young women know that they don't have to follow any sort of blueprint to fulfillment. You have the power to forge your own path and not accept the world the way it is. Experience a lot, write your own rules, and focus on the people and the little moments that ultimately bring you lasting joy.

WILD
FLOWER

Be ever growing, evolving, transforming, and becoming.

Every day we're growing, evolving, and changing. Just as wildflowers bloom through different seasons, we must welcome transition and trust that we too will establish our roots. Who we were yesterday is not who we are today and new experiences bring wisdom, clarity, and awaken our truest potential. Give yourself the space to try new opportunities even if they scare you. Not everything has to be perfect or permanent. All change brings opportunities for growth and transformation.

———— • ————

As you change and grow into the wildflower you are meant to be, you will find yourself outgrowing things, relationships, and situations that may not be serving you. Not everyone or everything that comes into your life is meant to stay. The best thing to learn is to *let go*. It's okay to outgrow romantic relationships when you realize you both want different things. It's okay to outgrow jobs where you don't feel personal or professional fulfillment. It's okay to outgrow friendships that are not healthy for you. It's okay to outgrow labels and stigmas that have made you feel pigeonholed into what you could become. To be a wildflower is to grow through those cracks in the cement, regardless of how hard it is to push through.

When you give yourself permission to be wild and grow freely, you don't let labels or expectations define you or keep you small. You grow into the woman of your own dreams, blooming far beyond what you had imagined. We are all capable of growth and expansion. We are always in a state of change, and we are all capable of creating the change we want to see in our lives.

You have room to grow no matter where you are in life. If you don't like your situation or you want more for yourself, you can do it. We are all wildflowers blooming into our next opportunity, our next transition. Ask yourself what you need to outgrow in order to become who you are meant to be. Perhaps it's imposter syndrome, an unhealthy relationship, or a limiting belief.

When things change inside you, things change around you. It is in our nature to crave change otherwise we stay stagnant and become unhappy. Transforming is where you want to be. You are always on your way to becoming a new you and are always evolving. Go after what you want with fierce determination and watch yourself bloom into the beautiful wildflower that you are.

And just as a wildflower needs tending to, require the same for yourself. Give yourself love, time, and attention. A wildflower doesn't grow overnight; it slowly expands into the beauty that it is. It blooms in light, and so do you.

"The best piece of advice

I've ever been given is stop doubting and just do it. No amount of preparation, education, or credentials will ever make you feel totally prepared. If you wait for perfection, you'll be waiting forever. That's why it is so important to push self-sabotaging thoughts to the side and take the risk, no matter how intimidating it might be."

ALICE PANIKIAN

*Miss Canada 2006, Founder of TheBronde.com,
and Advocate for Endometriosis Awareness
and Nontoxic Living*

AS A MODEL and former Miss Canada, Alice found herself immersed in the beauty industry in both her personal and her professional life. But, when Alice found herself in the throes of a painful disorder, her relationship with the products she was putting on her body changed forever.

In 2013, Alice was diagnosed with endometriosis. Upon doing research, Alice learned that excessive estrogen can worsen the disease and certain chemicals magnify estrogen's effect on the body. To her dismay, some of the very products she loved were causing her harm. In fact, she found that the beauty industry as a whole was astoundingly unregulated, and products often contained known carcinogens and hormone disruptors.

Alice has gone on to educate and raise awareness on the impact products have on our body. Despite the overwhelming amount of positive feedback she received from using her platform to teach others, she still felt the weight of imposter syndrome creeping in. For a long time, she let these voices of self-doubt cripple her ability to move forward, but the importance of her message pushed her to grow past these negative voices and lead with confidence. And this unwavering confidence helped lead her to success.

Allow yourself to grow beyond your own self-doubt. Jump in with the knowledge that you have something special to add to the conversation. Set yourself free to be the woman you want to be, and you will make your own impact on this world.

"I hope to live
a really long time—there
are hopes and dreams that I
have that I'm not even aware of
yet. Things I can't even envision yet.
It's invaluable to understand
that your path will eventually wind
and to feel comfort in that."

TRINITY MOUZON WOFFORD

Cofounder and CEO of Golde

TRINITY GREW UP in a single-parent household, with her mother battling an autoimmune disease. After her mother shifted to holistic health care to manage the symptoms of her disease, Trinity witnessed the life-changing benefits firsthand, and her interest in natural remedies and holistic healing was born.

Although the wellness industry had become increasingly more popular, Trinity noticed the market seemed overpriced and inaccessible for many demographics. Working together with her cofounder and partner, Issey Kobori, Trinity created Golde, superfood-infused products, with the mission to bring health and wellness essentials to the masses in a fun and inspired way.

With the success of Golde, Trinity often reflects on the experiences that brought her to this point. Growing up as one of the only Black families in her town, Trinity felt the burden and obligation to set a good example and prove people wrong when they didn't treat her with the respect she deserved. Ultimately, this fueled her determination to be successful. It's important to her, however, to find a balance between using moments of adversity and turning them into strengths, but not carrying them for too long so as not to perpetuate the negativity. This realization has been a huge point of growth for Trinity and has helped her blossom into the powerhouse that she is today.

Don't let adversity stop you from transforming into the person you are meant to be, but instead use it to fuel your determination and growth.

"I wouldn't tell my younger self anything—all of my life experiences have value. As challenging or as joyful as they are, **they build on one another.** A preview or sneak peek on how to live or what to do could cheat you out of experiences that are critical."

LO BOSWORTH

Founder and CEO of Love Wellness

AFTER STARRING IN hit reality shows *Laguna Beach* and *The Hills*, Lo found herself battling to outgrow the stigma and ideas around her reality TV persona. She dreamed of helping people and having a more meaningful impact on the world. She was passionate about cooking and was in talks with different networks to create a cooking show. Ultimately, these talks didn't amount to what Lo had hoped for.

This disappointment, combined with a terrible vitamin deficiency she was battling at the time, led to depression and health issues. While she worked to get a handle on her health, she discovered a passion for wellness and spreading awareness about holistic healing, and her company, Love Wellness, was born.

Love Wellness offers products developed and researched by doctors, food scientists, nutritionists, and holistic practitioners, specifically with women's biology and experience in mind. Whether it's Love Wellness products, or her passion for cooking, Lo has expanded far beyond the box that reality television had put her in. She attributes her different pursuits and successes to a "test and learn mind-set" and encourages other women not to corner themselves into one area.

When you don't limit yourself to the idea of one career or a singular focus, you may find your abilities just keep on growing. If something interests you, try it. You don't have to be just one thing. Keep evolving, and the sun will find you. Just like a wildflower, your colors will shine if you lean toward the light.

LIMIT
LESS

Let others' limiting beliefs about you fuel your fire to burn through them.

Limiting yourself is a learned behavior. We grow up hearing the word "can't" a lot. We have to actively unlearn limiting behaviors and reframe our mind-sets. When you don't have examples around you of people doing what you're doing, or don't have the financial support to start making your dream a reality, it's common to give up before you begin. Don't let limitations make you think that you can't achieve something. When you find yourself hitting a wall, it's easy to blame external forces.

———— • ————

We can think to ourselves, "I haven't gotten that promotion because my coworker has been here longer." "I haven't worked on my passion project because no one will take it seriously." "I haven't been investing in my friendships enough because we're all busy and focused on our careers." Instead of placing these feelings on things that are outside of your control, try this with me. Close your eyes. Say to yourself: "There's always time for what I put first" and "I can do anything I set my mind to." Really sit with that, and in this space, ask yourself: "What is my biggest dream? What life do I want to live? What mark do I want to leave on the world? What fuels my fire?"

My childhood encompassed a lot of financial struggle and instability. From a young age, I knew I didn't want a life of limitations. This desire to achieve more, have more, accomplish more, is a huge source of fuel that has helped me break through personal limitations. When self-doubt sets in, I remember what I'm working toward.

Your only limit is you, your mind. Unlearn what you've been told as a child. Break free of the limits placed on you. Build the life that *you* want to live. There is no one-size-fits-all career path—there are endless possibilities and opportunities out there if you are brave enough to seize them.

Living without limits means breaking boundaries and leaving your comfort zone behind. Believe that you can achieve something greater than what those around you are asking of you, or even what you are asking of yourself. When you have vision and purpose, the sheer force and expansion of your dreams will knock down any limiting beliefs that stand in your way.

When your vision and dream become bigger than your fear, you become limitless. You realize that it's always worth taking the risk. Even if it doesn't work out the way you intended, the growth and knowledge gained will push you in the right, and perhaps even better, direction. Abandon the fear and limits that are not serving you and inspire others to do the same.

"I find that in a
world that sets a lot of limits,
socially and mentally,
it is important to question things,
no matter your age or social condition.
It is essential to your growth. Values
and beliefs that you create through
your own personal experience are
what make you limitless."

NORA GHERBI

*Founder of WHo CAREs!? Chronicles, Board member of Edeyo Foundation,
Contributor to* Conscious Magazine

DIG DEEP AND question everything. This is the sentiment that Nora Gherbi shares with her daughter on the first day of school every year. After working as a senior trade and investment attaché, Nora began to notice an empty space in corporate strategies. This is when WHo CAREs!? Chronicles, a multimedia platform providing education and adequate resources for Corporate Social Responsibility (CSR) development, was born. By creating a new leading role, the Chief Care Officer, Nora has blazed the trail for executives and corporations to broaden their intention and positive impact on their communities and the world with partners including Cinq Etoiles Production, CFS Lablaco, changeNOW, Oceanic Global, and *Conscious* magazine.

Nora saw that companies were limiting their contributions to society through their lack of sustainability, transparency, and caring initiatives. As opposed to accepting this as just the way things are, she questioned it, looked beyond the scope of what has been, and envisioned what could be. See your limits not as a hindrance, but as an opportunity to imagine an even better solution.

Sometimes in life your greatest obstacles push you to your greatest heights. When you get creative, you can break the mold that has been set. By shattering the limits on your own thoughts and ingenuity you just may end up making the world a better place.

"Being limitless is
not letting others' judgments,
belittling comments, or questioning
of your ambitions deter you,
but rather propel you forward.
Trust your ability, your mind, and
your strength to be limitless and smash
through glass ceilings."

KRISSY MASHINSKY

Founder and CEO of usastrong.IO

AS A FORMER female executive, Krissy faced gender discrimination early on in her career. She found her decisions being questioned many more times as often as those of her male colleagues and criticized for behaviors they were rewarded for. In some cases, Krissy was even accused of trying to mask a lack of knowledge with her commanding energy. Not letting this criticism dictate the bounds of her success was an important part of navigating and succeeding in the business world. Krissy didn't allow her peers to limit what she could achieve. In order to break through, she had to put the trust in herself that others were not yet able to believe in or give, and show them the way.

Now, as the matriarch of a family with six children, a wife, and the cofounder and CEO of usastrong.IO, an online marketplace that verifies and curates USA-made products, Krissy has shown that a woman's place is anywhere she chooses to be.

Don't let criticism scare you into meekness. Be a woman who refuses limits. Lead by example and show the world what you're capable of. You may be knocking on that glass ceiling and feeling every day that you have to prove yourself. But once that glass shatters, no one can deny that you are exactly where you are supposed to be. Because a woman in her power is a woman with limitless potential.

"For me, being limitless is about letting your creative power unleash into the world without holding it back. It's about allowing yourself to move between boundaries and labels, and not letting fixed identities define you."

MAJO MOLFINO

Author of Break the Good Girl Myth
and Host of Heroine *Podcast*

AFTER WORKING AT a dead-end job in her early twenties that left her less than inspired, Majo found herself on a quest to redefine who she is and break the bounds of her own creativity. This process led her to discovering certain social structures that were holding her back. Majo earned a master's degree at Stanford University and authored *Break the Good Girl Myth*, a book focused on helping women define and move past the limits that have been preventing them from stepping into their full creative confidence.

For Majo, being limitless means allowing yourself to be a multidimensional, ever-evolving person. At age thirty, Majo changed her name. Her first name was María José. Changing her name meant reclaiming her heritage and both parts of her name, the "Ma" from María and the "Jo" from "José." Majo loves how it honors both the masculine and the feminine side to coexist simultaneously. This step allowed her to celebrate her growth and individuality.

By limiting our expression to fit into a box, we can, in turn, limit our ability to create and contribute to our personal and professional lives. It's important to not let boundaries and labels define us. You have the power to break free and become the best version of yourself. It all starts with delving inside, with an open heart and an open mind, and finding what makes you, you.

YOU'VE GOT THIS

Realize
your own potential
and become
unstoppable.

Self-doubt is inevitable. We all question at some point whether we have what it takes. Are we talented enough or are we special? Are we good enough or are we deserving? And the answer is you are. Trust that you can do the hard things. You are capable of overcoming whatever disappointments, setbacks, or heartbreaks come up. You have the power to accomplish whatever you set your mind to, and you deserve to live out your biggest dreams. My intuition has never misguided me. Deep down, we always know the right answers. Take in advice, but ultimately your path begins within.

Recall all the times you thought you couldn't get through something, and you figured out your way through. Think about all the times you doubted yourself and proved *yourself* wrong, the times you wanted to give up but kept going and where it led you. You've accomplished things before, and you will accomplish many more things ahead.

Change the negative thoughts into positive affirmations. The next time you catch yourself falling into the trap of questioning your abilities, close your eyes and say, "I can do this." Breathe it into existence. We become what we give our attention to. Make sure that when that attention is turned on you, it's full of love and gratitude. We are all more capable and qualified than we realize or give ourselves credit for.

Stop downplaying what you're doing—be loud and proud! Women in particular have the hardest time owning what we have to offer; society makes us feel that we're boastful or "too much" when we share our successes. Create accountability among your friends. Set goals and check in with each other. Celebrate each other's triumphs. It's important to pause and relish these moments, moments made all the sweeter when we are surrounded by our tribe.

Believe in yourself. Most of us have great ideas, but the difference between success and failure is *action*. Start with a simple question: What do you want and why do you want it? Success can mean so many things and it's your purpose in life to define what it means to *you*. Believe that you have the power to make it happen and get out of your own way. Would you rather have tried to make your dreams come true, or look back in twenty years with regret that you didn't take the leap? You are the author of your life. You choose what happens in your next chapter. What story will you write?

And the next time you question whether you have what it takes, remember . . . *you've got this.*

"Don't second-guess yourself too much. It's important to ask questions from the right people, but don't let the feedback destroy your vision."

CYNDI RAMIREZ-FULTON

Founder and CEO of Chillhouse

CYNDI HAS A GRIT that eventually landed her a job interview at *Vogue* magazine in her twenties. Despite *Vogue* being an iconic place to work, Cyndi was not sold on the idea of working for a big company. She still longed to forge her own path. The morning of her interview, she decided not to go and instead went full-steam ahead and launched her own business. Cyndi and her husband noticed a gap between the more antiquated, traditional spas and the modern millennial, and this became the seed of her empire, dawning her the Queen of Chill. Chillhouse has grown into a shining example of what a new-age spa can be, with the mission of easing you into the deepest form of self-care through trendy, updated services and a wellness cafe.

Growing up, Cyndi always admired Sophia Amoruso, the founder of Nasty Gal, a fashion empire, and Girlboss, a job marketplace for women. So imagine Cyndi's shock when Sophia messaged her on Instagram about getting involved with her business. This was a true manifestation moment and only the beginning of much success to come.

You don't have to start out knowing exactly what you're doing. You don't have to start out as the best. Just *start*. Ask for help, but don't let the opinions of others define your journey. It's okay to take time trying out different things in order to find your inspiration. You are exactly where you need to be.

"Literally, tell yourself out loud that you're up to your challenges. When you say something out loud, your subconscious believes **that it's true.**"

KRISTINA LOPEZ ADDUCI

Founder and CEO of House of Puff and Art Zealous

AS A LOVER OF ART and entertaining, Kristina has woven her passion into the fabric of her companies, Art Zealous, an arts media platform highlighting artists, trends, and events shaping the art world, and House of Puff, which is all about bringing elegance and a sense of luxury to the cannabis accessories market. By bringing beauty and femininity to a typically grungy and male-dominated industry, Kristina is working to destigmatize cannabis use for the modern working woman.

Growing up, Kristina had an exceptional role model in her strong Puerto Rican mother, who worked as a real estate agent when Kristina was young. As just a little girl, Kristina remembers asking her mother what she dreamed of being. When she replied that she wished she had become a doctor, Kristina responded with this: "If you dream that you can, you will." And her mother did. She studied tirelessly and became the doctor she had always dreamed of being.

This is something Kristina reflects on when she's struggling with the balance of raising her twins and being the CEO of her own company. When anxious thoughts seep in, she looks in the mirror and reminds herself that she's got this.

Follow in the footsteps of the women you admire. Don't be afraid to be scrappy. Be willing to put in the time to make your dreams work. And remember, no matter what challenges you face, you have the power inside you to conquer them.

"Navigating the male-dominated
high-tech world as a woman and mother
is full of obstacles, but having the confidence
to know that 'I've got this' when faced with
each one of these challenges has
always pulled me through."

MING NG

Principal Data Scientist of HackerOne

MALE CLASSMATES AND male professors in a male-dominated field: walking into her computer science courses in college left Ming feeling intimidated at first. Instead of allowing herself to dwell on feeling like a fish out of water, she put her attention on the work, and her hard work paid off.

Ming was recruited by a top company during her final year of undergrad and went on to receive her master's in computer science. Ming worked for the company that recruited her up until the birth of her twins. During maternity leave, Ming wondered how she would ever return to work. When it finally felt like the right time, she asked the company to come back as a part-time employee. No other engineers at the company worked part time, but because of Ming's talent they reluctantly granted her wish. The catch was that she would lose her health insurance, which she anticipated, and her pay would be reduced, which she did not anticipate. As opposed to working for less than her worth, Ming declined their offer with no fallback in the wings. Within a month, though, Ming was hired part time at another company, doing a more interesting job, with even higher pay.

A deep breath and an inward "you've got this" has been Ming's way of dealing with the surprises and hurdles that come up in life. Your ability to succeed starts with your belief that you have the capacity to accomplish anything, that you've got this.

CONTRIBUTOR LIST

Live Inspired
Robbie Brenner
Dianna Cohen
Amber Vittoria

Be Bold
Connie Lim, a.k.a MILCK
Jodie Patterson
Mandana Dayani

Self Love
Gaylyn Henderson
Dani Candray
Jessica Iacullo

Say Yes
Taylor Schilling
Susan Rockefeller
Meghan Asha

Live Fearlessly
Amanda Nguyen
Jessica Ekstrom
Miki Agrawal

Keep Aiming
Stacy London
Eliza Blank
Cameron Armstrong

Embrace Change
Natasha Huang Smith
Kelsie Hayes
Dana Pollack

Trailblazer
Amanda Lepore
Sharon Isbin
Lauren Singer

Move Mountains
Becky Straw
Allie Brudner
Amy Ziff

Ride the Wave
Lea d'Auriol
Lindsey Metselaar
Essa O'Shea

Heart of Gold
Roberta Annan
Heather Hartnett
Adriana Carrig

Powerful
Emily Warren
Rooshy Roy
Elizabeth Beisel

Hustle
Ali Kriegsman
Dani Egna
Parker Bowie Larson

Perseverance
Tianna Bartoletta
Veronica Webb
Gabriela Hearst

Unbreakable
Sarah Larson Levey
Heidi Kristoffer
Julia Broglie

Wing Woman
Lisa Mayer
Katya Libin
Lisa Rosado

Think Positive
Larissa Thomson
Janet MacGillivray
Michelle Cordeiro Grant

Wildflower
Alice Panikian
Trinity Mouzon Wofford
Lo Bosworth

Limitless
Nora Gherbi
Krissy Mashinsky
Majo Molfino

You Got This
Cyndi Ramirez-Fulton
Kristina Lopez Adduci
Ming Ng